# VALUES BASED ORGANIZATIONS

# VALUES BASED ORGANIZATIONS

## ALIGNING CULTURE AND STRATEGY

## DR. THOMAS EPPERSON

**||| INNERWILL**
M E D I A

VALUES BASED ORGANIZATIONS
*Aligning Culture and Strategy*

FIRST EDITION

ISBN    978-1-5445-4920-0  *Hardcover*

978-1-5445-4919-4  *Paperback*

978-1-5445-4918-7  *Ebook*

978-1-5445-4921-7  *Audiobook*

# Contents

# Introduction

The company failed.

Hundreds laid off. Equipment silent, waiting to be sold. Customers scrambling to find new suppliers. Vendors holding outstanding bills. Employees stunned and scared and wondering what comes next.

Nothing guarantees that organizations will thrive or even survive. Every day, businesses dissolve under their own hubris. We think it can't happen to us, and when it does, shock comes first followed by blame and resignation. Sometimes markets turn and we cannot adapt; other times our luck runs out and things don't go our way. We make bad choices or allow a toxic culture to fester under our watch. And then the business goes away.

As leaders, we have a responsibility to look ahead. To anticipate, to adapt. To align our organizations around compelling ideas, and to build workforces who have the will and skill to execute on them. We have a responsibility to use every tool in our toolbox to influence, motivate, and occasionally cajole our teams in support of a plan to win.

Win, and we win together. Lose, and we face consequences. More than paychecks, our organizations provide careers, development, and community for our people. When led well, with courage and compassion, they make a positive impact in the world. When led poorly, they do harm, consuming money and hope.

As leaders we have a responsibility to do better, to be better, and to create the kind of organizations where employees, customers, and stakeholders thrive. Where people achieve amazing things. The kind of organizations that do good and do well.

This book is about how to build organizations that thrive—Values Based Organizations whose cultures support their strategies, and whose strategies inspire their cultures. It describes the leadership required to build alignment throughout an organization, starting with the senior leaders and influencing frontline employees. Based on real organizations that have achieved fantastic results, this book details a process for building a Values Based Organization of your own.

As an organizational leader, you may want to develop a strategic plan. This book gives you a process to do so. You may want to strengthen your culture. It will give you examples to follow. You may sense that your leaders are not on the same page and have different goals. This book can help you bring them together.

The goal of this book is to help leaders build better, more effective organizations who in turn have a positive impact on the lives of their employees and communities. It does not matter if your organization is for-profit, nonprofit, or a state or federal agency. The principles apply in any organization where you can define the future you want to create. The principles apply to organizations of all sizes, from teams to companies to multinationals, although the larger the organization, the bigger the challenge of alignment becomes. Finally, the principles apply to any organizational leader who has the influence and grit to make it so.

Meant to be practical, this book is grounded in research and in real-world experiences, honed by real people doing real work on their organizations over many years. It is rooted in a fourth-generation family business—Luck Companies—and all the leaders who have transformed the organization into one of the most highly engaged workplaces in the United States. This book is not meant to be a textbook or a scientific document, although it draws inspiration from both and content from leaders, authors, and thinkers in a variety of industries, as well as clients and board members from our leadership institute. It includes interviews with:

- Bob Kelley, former COO of Ukrop's Supermarkets and President of Pure Culture
- Chris Yates, head of talent for multiple Fortune 500 companies in technology and manufacturing
- Meagan Metzger, CEO of Dcode
- John Pullen, Chief Growth Officer of Luck Companies
- Charlie Luck, CEO of Luck Companies
- Guy Clumpner, President of Holt Development Services, Inc.
- Dr. Jerry Burch and Dr. Jana Burch of the University of West Florida

- Scott Evans, CEO, and Kristin Ogo, COO, of Kenmore Envelope
- Brian Law, CEO of Law Family Companies

As for me, I grew up working in multiple failed family businesses: over the years we had a sawmill, heavy equipment shop, farm, construction firm, electrical contracting company, a backwoods business park, and a handful of half-baked ideas including a cider business, a wine making operation that may or may not have started as a still in the woods, and some "easy money" land deals. Aside from hard work, an overdeveloped sense of independence, and poverty, I came away with a belief that I can do almost anything with enough effort, and so can you. I understand what's at stake when we win, and what's at stake when we fail. I've seen what happens when a business goes bankrupt, when we put people out of work, when equipment sits idle, waiting to be sold. I've been part of a toxic culture and been led by narcissistic leaders; I know what it's like to live in a house with no paycheck and little hope.

On top of my personal experience, for over twenty-five years, I've helped lead the cultural transformation of hundreds of organizations and thousands of leaders that InnerWill has supported across the United States. This book draws on that knowledge and experience, from countless industries, types of organizations, and styles of leadership.

The book is organized around the Five Practices of Values Based Organizations. You will find examples, stories, quotes, and exercises that will help your organization become more aligned and more effective. This book is meant to be easy to read and can be lighthearted at times, although the work of organizations is often serious and challenging.

This book is not filled with easy answers but is full of practical advice. The Five Practices are meant to be simple; applying them consistently is hard, given how many distractions and how little time organizations seem to have. If these practices were easy, every leader would do them, and in my experience, few do. The practices result in outcomes organizations want—like successfully executed strategies, cultures that create value for stakeholders, and a positive impact on the lives of employees, but few organizations choose to invest the time, energy, and perseverance required. The Five Practices of Values Based Organizations work if you do the work.

This book exists because of all the organizational leaders who came before—facilitating, sweating, and striving to build the best organizations possible. It has contributions from many people, all of whom I am incredibly grateful for. To all of those who have shared their time and wisdom with our team, thank you.

Finally, this book is about you and your choices. On our team, our board, and in our parent company, we believe that leadership focused on the success of others will make things better in our workplaces, our communities, and in our families. That positive impact is our ultimate goal. Through the practices of Values Based Organizations, we want to develop better people, braver leaders, and a wiser world.

Thank you for reading, and more importantly, thank you for the positive impact you will have on your organization, employees, and communities.

# Prologue

Imagine the gears in an engine, out of alignment, grinding together, missing and spitting, and jerking the car to a halt.

Envision a group of rowers, all pulling at different speeds and in different directions.

Picture an orchestra where the players play different songs at different tempos and volumes while the conductor is nowhere to be seen.

Visualize a sports team where everyone follows a different playbook and doesn't understand what position they play.

These images describe the typical organization: unclear on where they are going, why they are going there, and what they want to accomplish.

Now imagine an organization that has a clear mission explaining why it exists. Whose culture supports the outcomes of its strategic plan. Whose vision inspires employees to think big and work toward a common goal. An organization with leaders who model similar behaviors, actively influence teams to work together, and despite having strong opinions, publicly commit to the organization's goals. Processes that make sense and enable the culture, strategy, and leaders. An organization with employees who understand their goals, act on the values of the organization, and contribute to something larger than themselves.

This is not a typical organization. It is rare—even unicorn-like. Having this level of extreme alignment is possible, but it takes leadership and influence, hard work, and processes. It takes people with the will and skill to see the alignment through, who don't settle for mediocrity, who don't make excuses, who focus on a few priorities, and who don't tolerate terrible leaders running roughshod across their teams.

You wouldn't build an engine that misfires constantly, field a sports team that has no positions, or listen to an orchestra playing different songs in different keys simultaneously. So why do we settle for organizations that have no stated mission, no clear goals for the future, and no plan to get there other than to do more with less but faster? Organizations whose culture holds them hostage, and keeps them from achieving greatness? Organizations whose leaders couldn't hit water if they fell out of a boat? And employees so disengaged they drag their feet counting the minutes to quitting time, then retirement?

Our organizations don't have to be this way. We can choose a different path, a path that runs in a straight line between mission to values, vision to strategy, and leadership to process. We can build organizations that make sense. Organizations that run well.

And it all starts with a choice.

# CHAPTER ONE

# Values Based Organizations

Why do Values Based Organizations matter?

Values Based Organizations exhibit strong alignment between their strategy, culture, and processes while encouraging employees at all levels to act on the organization's goals.

The Five Practices of Values Based Organizations have their origins in Luck Companies, a fourth-generation family business with a history of over one hundred years. The organization is in the rock business—construction aggregates for the most part. As employees like to say, "We take big rocks and make them into small rocks and dig big holes in the ground." Located throughout the Southeastern United States, Luck is one of the largest privately held and operated stone businesses in the country.

In the 1990s, Luck experienced rapid growth: the company tripled in size, tripled in footprint, and tripled in revenue. As a family business, the leadership of Luck Companies also shifted from Charles S. Luck III to Charles S. Luck IV. Amidst these changes, Luck needed to modernize how it did business. The company had grown too complex to manage in a command-and-control manner; and so, the company decentralized, establishing regions and executives who could be closer to customers.

However, the company did not consider the impact these changes would have on the organization's culture, or the leadership needed in the new environment. Despite so many decent, hardworking people, the culture grew more toxic and combative, with managers arguing over resources, customers, and decisions. In a time when collaboration came at a premium, the executive team played politics with one another while jockeying for power. The company's multiple regions did not work together to create an excellent experience for customers or vendors, forcing others to adapt their approaches to the company's inconsistent processes. Even with a long history of doing the right thing, and leading with high integrity, the company struggled with a new, and unwelcome, culture. These conflicts spread through the employee population as turnover and dissatisfaction increased. By the early 2000s employees began to whisper that the company had lost its way.

Frustrated by conflict within his executive team, Chief Executive Officer Charlie Luck directed the HR Vice President to work with him to find a consultant to help. The company tried out several—they would come in with slick suits and team-building gimmicks, and each one failed against the executives' dysfunction and misalignment. Finally, one of Luck's partners, Caterpillar, recommended that Luck speak with the Holt Caterpillar, one of the largest Caterpillar dealers in the United States, who had suffered from similar problems but who had turned things around using an approach called Values Based Leadership ("VBL").

Inspired by the book *Managing By Values* by Blanchard and O'Connor (2003), Holt had been practicing their own version of Values Based Leadership for five years and sent Luck one of their executives, Guy Clumpner. With his pointed cowboy boots and his tight black shirt, Guy strode into a room filled with Luck executives who had not been leading in alignment for years. He started with a single request: "Write down everything that is wrong with this company." Given their animosity toward one another, they furiously filled one sheet after another until Guy said, "Put down your pencils. Who wrote down 'me'?"

Somehow, it worked. For the first time, the leadership team looked in the mirror and recognized that any change they wanted to make had to start with them. After that experience, the company got serious about the culture it wanted to create by choosing the four values that define it to this day: integrity, commitment, creativity, and leadership. The executive team began to work on themselves and their leadership first and foremost. After eighteen months of work, they rolled the organization's values and leadership expectations out to the organization, launched an intensive leadership development program, and began to hold themselves and others accountable.

Not everything worked. In the early years of the values journey, Luck experimented with a wide variety of approaches: retreats, workshops, mentoring, leadership 360 surveys, various tools, conversation starters, weekly meetings, VBL coaches, leadership index scores, and engagement surveys. Several senior-level leaders did not have the will or the skill to do the work and left the company. Others found too much of a gap between the company's aspirations and what happened in reality and resigned on their own. The company had starts and stops, periods of an intense focus on leadership, and periods of focusing more on the operations side of the business. However, despite the setbacks, employees made enough progress to continue to invest in the work.

Over the next several years, the company's values and leadership evolution grew more refined. Customers, vendors, and other stakeholders benefited from a much more effective and financially successful company, while employee engagement scores grew to become some of the highest in the country. Employees began to tell stories of how they took the leadership skills they learned at work home with them—an unexpected benefit—and talked about becoming better parents, siblings, and even soccer coaches. Under Charlie's leadership, the work continues to this day.

A major milestone in the company's evolution occurred in 2008 when the construction industry collapsed. A majority of the company's revenues evaporated, and Charlie Luck grew ill. As the company struggled to stay afloat, eventually reducing the company's headcount by half, Charlie struggled to get out of bed and get back on his feet. Over the course of his illness, he asked all the big questions: What is happening to me? What will happen to the company? If I survive this, what will be different?

By 2009 the economy, the company, and Charlie's health had stabilized, and when he came back to work, he made an announcement: the company would stand for more than just making money—the company would make a positive impact in the world. At the time, he did not know how Luck would do that but set the organization on a path to figure it out.

As part of this challenge, the company developed a new mission—to ignite human potential. Building on a foundation of caring for people, the company made the explicit connection between doing good and doing well—the company could have a positive impact on the lives of others and make money. As part of its mission, the company decided to share what it had learned about culture, leadership, and family business outside of its walls, leading to the creation of the InnerWill Leadership Institute and the Five Practices of Values Based Organizations.

Values Based Organizations use a set of well-defined values to guide how the organization operates. Values Based Organizations have developed the following components:

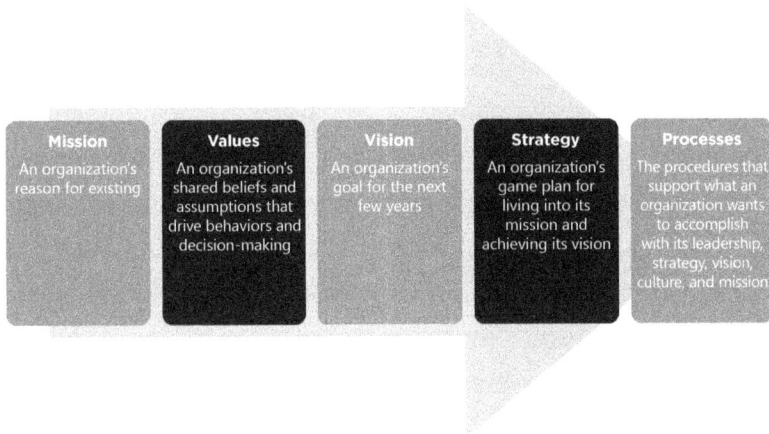

| Mission | Values | Vision | Strategy | Processes |
|---------|--------|--------|----------|-----------|
| An organization's reason for existing | An organization's shared beliefs and assumptions that drive behaviors and decision-making | An organization's goal for the next few years | An organization's game plan for living into its mission and achieving its vision | The procedures that support what an organization wants to accomplish with its leadership, strategy, vision, culture, and mission |

In addition to defining these aspects of the organization, Values Based Organizations have developed the leadership horsepower they need to lead with values, execute on their strategy, deliver on their mission and vision, and ensure that they have the necessary processes in place. Leaders in Values Based Organizations create alignment across the enterprise—not just by defining these principles, but by influencing the organization to act on them as well. Again and again and again and again. Employees in an organization are like paddlers in a canoe...if everyone rows together, the boat glides through the water. If everyone rows at different tempos and gives wildly different amounts of effort, at best the boat careens from one spot to another, and at worst dumps them all in the water. Leaders in Values Based Organizations get the right people in the boat, teach them how to paddle, and get everybody rowing. They set the course, motivating the paddlers to give the optimal amount of effort. They create alignment.

Alignment is one of the key drivers of Values Based Organizations—because most things run better in alignment. A chiropractor would say your body runs better when your spine is aligned. A mechanic would say your car runs better when the wheels are aligned. Your dentist would say your kids' teeth chew better when their teeth are aligned. A lack of alignment within organizations creates inefficiency and wasted effort, crossed purposes and failed strategies. We have all been on teams where no one worked together, where no one knew how to win or what winning even meant. The root causes of a lack of alignment within organizations are numerous—no defined mission, values, vision, or strategy, processes that drive outcomes unrelated to larger goals, a lack of leadership, leadership fighting for themselves and not for each other, unclear decision-making and expectations, and a lack of communication and coordination.

Leading to create alignment does not assume everything will stay the same—it assumes that things change and evolve as the environment does. Each organization needs just enough structure to allow consistency and space to adapt. In the field of organizational development, experts call it a loose/tight model—some things you make exceptionally clear, and other things you keep open and undefined. The magic in modern organizations is figuring out which should be which. In Values Based Organizations, leaders keep mission, values, vision, strategy, leadership expectations, and critical processes tight and well-articulated. This approach allows employees to adapt to stakeholders and each other as the need arises. Harley-Davidson described this approach as freedom with fences. In this case, the fences are defined, and as long as employees act inside of the boundaries set by the strategy, they have freedom to act.

Values Based Organizations exist in every type of category—for profit, nonprofit, government agency, family owned, or publicly held—and in every industry, from power generation to finance to construction. Leaders can build Values Based Organizations at any stage in the life cycle of an organization—at the founding and startup phases, in growth and scaling phases, in mature oldline businesses, or in young, rapidly evolving niches. Their fences may be tighter, or their freedom may be looser, but Values Based Organizations have several practices in common.

**Five Practices of**

# VALUES-BASED ORGANIZATIONS

**TAKE STOCK**
Seeing the organization clearly
- Assess what's working and what's not
- Seek feedback
- Measure progress

**ENGAGE EVERYONE**
Inspiring employee commitment
- Encourage leadership at all levels
- Energize employees with direction & support
- Empower employees to make a difference

**COMMIT TO WHY AND HOW**
Establishing the culture
- Refine the mission
- Operationalize the values
- Clarify expectations

**CHAMPION VALUES-BASED LEADERSHIP**
Inspiring organization commitment
- Develop leadership strength
- Influence key people
- Hold self and others accountable

**ALIGN ACTIONS**
Influencing the organization
- Evolve a vision and strategy
- Strengthen relationships
- Improve core processes

**INNERWILL**
LEADERSHIP INSTITUTE

## FIVE PRACTICES OF VALUES BASED ORGANIZATIONS

To build and maintain Values Based Organizations, follow these Five Practices:

1. Take Stock
2. Commit to Why and How

3. Align Action
4. Champion Values Based Leadership
5. Engage Everyone

**Taking Stock** means seeing the organization clearly. To do so, we:

- Assess what is working and what is not
- Seek feedback
- Measure progress

Taking Stock requires a candid and thoughtful review of the facts in an organization—with as clear a view as possible, assessing an organization's strengths, weaknesses, opportunities, and threats. The process collects data on the organization from inside and out, preferably from key stakeholders including leaders, employees, customers, and vendors. The data itself should include a combination of hard numbers—quantitative data like revenue, margins, or costs—and qualitative data, in other words, the stories that bring the hard numbers to life.

**Committing to Why and How** means establishing the desired culture. To do so, we:

- Refine our mission
- Operationalize our values
- Clarify expectations

Committing to Why and How helps establish why an organization exists—its mission—and how it chooses to operate—its values. The Why and How of an organization provide clear examples of how to treat others, including customers, employees, or the community. The Why and How provide a filter for making decisions that support alignment within the organization.

**Aligning Action** means influencing the organization. To do so, we:

- Evolve our vision and strategy
- Strengthen relationships
- Improve core processes

Aligning Action gets everyone in an organization on the same page and acting in a way that supports shared goals. To create this outcome, organizations need a vision for the future—an overarching goal guiding the organization for a number of years—and a strategy or game plan for achieving this goal. Alignment also requires healthy relationships within teams and across departments, since relationships often impact outcomes. To support aligned action, organizations also need processes that support the organization's goals.

**Championing Values Based Leadership** means inspiring organizational commitment. To do so, we:

- Develop leadership strength
- Influence key people
- Hold self and others accountable

Values Based Organizations require leaders to use values to make decisions and drive results. They develop themselves and others with the people and technical skills required for the future. They influence stakeholders and have a positive impact on employees.

To champion Values Based Leadership, formal leaders provide a high degree of clarity on their expectations, as well as feedback on performance, followed by rewards and consequences—in other words, accountability.

**Engaging Everyone** means inspiring employee commitment. To do so, we:

- Engage leadership at all levels
- Energize employees with direction and support
- Empower employees to make a difference

To inspire employee commitment, leaders need to Engage Everyone, encouraging them to lean into the organization's mission, values, vision, and strategy. With everyone making leadership choices, Values Based Organizations provide employees with the direction and support they need to do their best work. When employees have the tools and resources they need and feel called to do so, they make a significant impact on organizational outcomes.

The Five Practices of Values Based Organizations work interdependently; they grow more effective when used together. For example, an organization may develop a strategic plan as part of Aligning Action, but if it does not clarify its values by Committing to Why and How, the culture may undermine the strategy. While there is a natural order to the practices, starting with Taking Stock and finishing with Engaging Everyone, an organization's situation determines the best first step. If a business lacks the leadership horsepower it needs to move the organization, the business may need to start with Championing Values Based Leadership. If an organization already has well-defined values that everyone knows and acts on, it does not need to completely overhaul them during the next strategic planning session.

Not every organization takes the time to develop a strategy, or even an annual plan and budget. Those that do typically conduct a retreat for a few days in a hotel, develop a nice binder that they then place on a shelf until the next planning retreat. Leaders using these Five Practices recognize that this process does not stop—it may speed up or slow down, it may skip an action or two, but the practices continue throughout the life of the organization. Hence the name "practices" and not "steps."

By following the Five Practices of Values Based Organizations, leaders strengthen alignment within their organizations, which results in better outcomes like more engaged employees or a consistent customer experience. Depending on the type of organization, these outcomes can lead to increased revenue, better service, or a successful mission.

### KEY TAKEAWAYS

To follow the Five Practices of Values Based Organizations, we:

1. Take Stock
2. Commit to Why and How
3. Align Action
4. Champion Values Based Leadership
5. Engage Everyone

# CHAPTER TWO

# Take Stock

Why does Taking Stock matter?

To develop a plan for the future, you need to know who you are and where you have been.

In the late 1980s and 1990s, Bob Kelley worked for Ukrop's Super Markets, ultimately serving in the Chief Operating Officer role. Over time, Ukrop's became one of the most innovative super-market chains in the country. The company was one of the first companies to offer prepared foods, sushi, loyalty cards, and banking in their stores. Known for its high-service culture, Ukrop's attracted grocery executives from all over the country to learn how the company did business.

Strategy, according to Bob, starts with mindset readiness. How open are senior leaders to leaving behind their former paradigms to embrace new ideas? At Ukrop's, the owners of the company, Jim and Bobby Ukrop, wanted to experiment with new approaches and allowed Bob and other senior leaders to chase ideas as part of strategic planning. For example, in 1986 Jim Ukrop read a food industry research paper that said only 13 percent of couples knew what they were having for dinner when they left work. This insight led to Ukrop's offering prepared foods. Sushi followed a more difficult path: when Bob brought the idea back from a market in Seattle, the organization's leadership balked. "No one is going to buy sushi in Richmond," they said. Bob persevered, and today sushi is one of the most profitable supermarket products, while Kroger is currently the largest sushi provider in the United States. Without a readiness to change, leaders struggle to imagine the future they could create and find difficulty in executing an innovative strategy.

Bob himself struggled when Jim Ukrop came to Bob and asked him to start a bank. "I can't even get the bags packed right. Now you want me to run a bank?" It took a field trip to Omaha, Nebraska, watching bank employees in a supermarket easily connect with customers that it clicked for Bob. Soon Ukrop's had a billion in assets in their very own bank.

For an innovative strategy to be successful, leaders need to understand the connection between behaviors, strategy, and brand. At Ukrop's, one simple behavior predicted the strength of their customer service: leading customers to products. Bob sent secret shoppers into their stores to measure how often associates would lead customers to the green beans or sliced almonds. If associates did it 96 percent of the time, leaders at Ukrop's considered it successful. Anything less meant they had not achieved the cultural outcomes, strategy, or brand experience they wanted.

Bob has found that many senior leaders have a fixed mindset rather than the growth mindset demonstrated by the Ukrops brothers. "The problem with CEOs who have a fixed mindset," says Bob, is that "they don't believe in the relationship between a behavior and performance." They don't believe that employees have that much of an impact on their brand, or even the execution of their strategy. They believe that they can just say, "Be more productive," and their underlings will make it happen. According to Bob, only three out of ten CEOs have the conviction necessary to execute at such a high level. "They aren't trained for it. They personally don't care or they're not willing to do what's necessary to make it happen."

In some workplaces, taking an honest and hard look at the organization's strengths and weaknesses feels taboo. Employees worry about what leaders will do if they learn their baby is ugly. (And no, saying, "What a baby!" or "That baby sure is unique!" or "Too bad he looks like his father" are not Taking Stock.) Leaders feel that if their organization has flaws, or more importantly has flaws they care about, that somehow those flaws reflect on them as people. Shareholders punish anything less than good news—many will forgive a variety of sins if the organization grows and makes money, until they don't. Communities provide organizations with a social license to operate and have the power to put those organizations out of business if they step too far out of bounds once too often. The stakes feel high.

Worried about our own insecurities, we prevent our organizations from looking in the mirror. Fear keeps us from talking openly about how we are amazing and where we fall short. Every organization has strengths, or it would not exist. Every organization has weaknesses because perfection is a myth. And organizations are made up of people, who at the best of times are messy works in progress.

Leaders in Values Based Organizations understand the value of honesty and feedback, and they do not punish people for telling the truth. They know they must evolve over time; they realize accurate feedback and intentional choices speed this evolution along.

The world—including markets, products, people, technology, and culture—constantly evolves. Things change. In this environment, if organizations do not evolve, they will not survive. Blockbuster did not survive Netflix sending DVDs through the mail, which ultimately led to streaming platforms. While they invented the digital camera in the 1970s, Kodak barely survived the rise of digital photography and cameras in our phones. There is still a lone Blockbuster store in Oregon, and the Eastman Kodak Company still has revenues close to $1 billion. Bed Bath and Beyond's ever-present coupons and delightfully overpacked stores did nothing to help it tackle the modern landscape of online purchases. Combined with overwhelming debt, the company could not hope to adapt fast enough to outrun its creditors. Even when a company is a darling of Silicon Valley, with a new take on an old model—WeWork's focus on filling long-term lease commercial space with short-term co-working clients—does not protect it from the vagaries of demand and the market. These organizations may rise again, but they are case studies of how the world moves on, and if we do not, the world is content to move on without us.

Values Based Organizations operate in the polarity of stability and evolution—hanging on to what is great about their culture and operations, while actively experimenting and evolving as their markets do. In order to evolve effectively, organizations must understand the current state of the organization before leaping into the future. To do so, leaders Take Stock using three actions:

- Assessing what is working and what is not
- Seeking feedback
- Measuring progress

## ASSESSING WHAT IS WORKING AND WHAT IS NOT

Leaders have numerous ways of assessing what is working and what is not: having a robust discussion about financials and operations, revenue, and people. Playing golf with customers and eventually asking about the business. Huddling in a conference room to pore over spreadsheets. Wandering job sites, checking to see if anyone left their equipment idling, lost track of tools, or fell asleep on a pile of drywall.

One of the simplest ways of assessing what is working and what is not is to conduct a SWOT analysis. SWOT stands for Strengths, Weaknesses, Opportunities, and Threats; the model provides a framework for reflecting on the current state of an organization. Developed sometime during the 1960s and '70s, either at Harvard or Stanford, perhaps by a man called Albert Humphrey—no one is really sure—SWOT analysis focuses participants on the internal strengths of an organization, the internal weaknesses of an organization, the external opportunities for an organization, and the external threats of an organization.

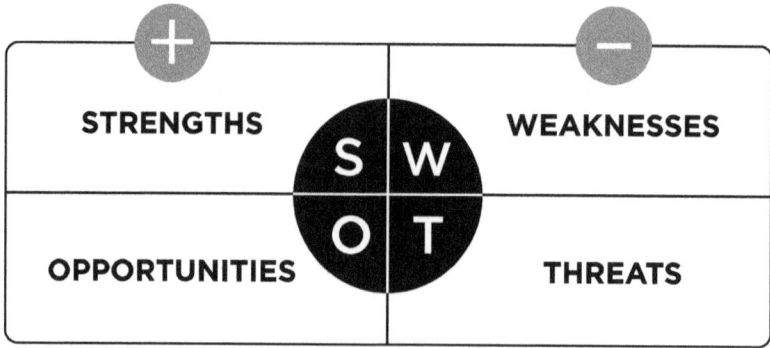

As you conduct your SWOT, reflect on the various aspects of your organization. For example, areas like:

- Revenue
- Margins
- Costs
- People
- Processes
- Culture
- Competitors
- Products
- Technology
- Service
- Operational efficiency
- Innovation

To start, consider the strengths of the organization. Focus on areas that are internal, that the organization has control of and the ability to influence. Strengths could be superior products or services, incredible talent, or a business with high barriers to entry. Try and move past generalities such as, "People are our greatest strength" and toward more specific examples such as,

"We have a talent pipeline to the top engineering schools in the Midwest." Some questions you may ask are:

1. What are the strengths of this organization?
2. How do we compete in the marketplace for sales, customers, talent, or supplies?
3. Why do customers/donors/stakeholders stay with us?
4. What is awesome about our culture and our people?
5. What is our secret sauce?

When it comes to strengths, it is helpful to distill the essence of your organization—why people join you, what makes you unique, what special value you create for customers, etc.—whatever reason you win, and try to describe it as clearly as you can. The essence of your organization matters because you will want to take this secret sauce and leverage it in the future. You should also be aware that what you think your secret sauce is might not be so secret, and it might not be so saucy. You might be wrong and fall in love with the wrong aspect of your business.

For example, leaders at Luck Companies believed that customers cared about quality above all and that quality was its secret sauce. The company invested millions in operations that could produce high-quality construction aggregates for use in asphalt and concrete. After the turndown in 2008 and the slow recovery in 2009, the company realized it needed a new strategic plan. Part of that plan required the company to talk directly to customers. Confident that customers would reaffirm the belief that quality was its competitive advantage, leaders brought in several of the largest customers who all said the same thing, "As long as your stone is in spec, we don't care." Luck, it seems, had fallen in love with the wrong thing. Quality was not the company's secret sauce.

Another aspect of an organization's strengths includes its core competencies: what does the company do really well? Ukrop's core competencies included customer service. Walmart excels at logistics. Disney Theme Parks says their core competencies focus on creating magic moments for guests, yet according to some employees, operational efficiency is their true core competency. Understanding core competencies can help predict what strategies the company will excel at in the future, especially if they extend the existing strengths of the business. However, understanding core competencies can help predict what strategies the company will struggle with, especially if the strategies require new core competencies. According to Bob Kelley, although innovation formed part of Ukrop's core competencies, using data to make decisions did not. When they launched the first customer loyalty card, they collected reams of data but did not use it to guide the operations, purchasing, and customer experience within their stores.

After strengths, consider the weaknesses of the organization. Focus on areas that are internal, that the organization has control of and the ability to influence. Again, move past generalities like "cash flow" and toward more specificity such as, "Eighty percent of our key customers are incredibly price sensitive and have plenty of other options to choose from." Some questions you may ask are:

1. What are the weaknesses of this organization?
2. How do our competitors compete in the marketplace for sales, customers, talent, or supplies?

3. Why do customers/donors/stakeholders leave us?
4. In what areas do our people struggle?
5. What is our greatest vulnerability?

When it comes to weaknesses, most of us are fairly proud of what we do. Otherwise, we wouldn't do it. Our pride can blind us to what makes our competitors awesome. Remember, they are proud of what they do, too. And they still exist, so they must be doing something right. Our pride can also blind us to our own shortcomings. And since there is no such thing as the perfect organization, chances are you have some weaknesses that you could improve on. Just because you have weaknesses does not mean you have a terrible organization—remember, you don't have to be bad to be better. Much like distilling your secret sauce, it is helpful to understand the difference between something that is good enough versus something that is a weakness that could hamper the organization. Sure, maybe you have ten-year-old laptops that can't run the latest software, but is that weakness as potentially damaging as all of your key talent retiring in two years when you have no succession plan?

In 2010, one of the greatest weaknesses Luck Companies uncovered during its strategy work stemmed from a lack of consistency between operations. Customers would drive around with binders detailing all the different ways the company sold and loaded stone materials. The company made it hard for customers to do business between regions and even locations. Before 2010, the culture did not drive consistency or simplicity. That weakness had to be shored up as part of any strategic plan.

After identifying the strengths and weaknesses of the organization, consider opportunities. Focus on areas that are external to the organization, which provide a chance to grow, expand market share, earn new customers, offer more services, or improve the organization's capabilities. Opportunities tend to be things you may have considered in the past but have not yet taken advantage of, or they may be totally new ideas. These can be small opportunities—such as increasing pricing by 3 percent—or larger opportunities such as a potential acquisition. Some questions you may ask are:

1. What opportunities can this organization take?
2. In what areas can we expand, grow, or take advantage of?
3. What could we do that would help the organization?
4. How could we use our secret sauce?
5. How can we add new customers or sell more to existing customers?

Opportunities, and the work to take advantage of them, are infinite. You can do anything you like with enough time, talent, and money. Unfortunately, most of us don't have unlimited talent or money, and time is the one thing we can't get more of. As you consider your organization's opportunities, it is helpful to narrow them down to realistic actions given your constraints—how much time, talent, and money do you have to invest in this effort? What are a few things you could do exceptionally well, as opposed to doing a great number of things halfway? More importantly, what opportunities build on your secret sauce (that thing that makes you special)?

Leaders can use the following comparison—the relationship of value, risk, and effort—to determine whether to take advantage of an opportunity.

**↑ VALUE   ↓ RISK   ↓ EFFORT**

From Tom Koulopoulos, Delphi Group

Ideally, opportunities should bring high value to the organization, with minimal risk and effort. Opportunities like these are few and far between. More likely, every opportunity will have a mix of value, risk, and effort to implement them, and people *will* disagree with these estimates. One of the most effective conversations leaders can have when considering opportunities includes a discussion about the value, risk, and effort different opportunities provide and facilitating agreement between leaders on this equation.

Over the past several years, carmakers have had to weigh the value, risk, and effort of moving toward wholly electric vehicles (EVs). They had to weigh the consumer interest, costs of production, available technology, infrastructure, and government incentives and regulations. While electric vehicles have been around since the 1830s, beginning with the first electric carriage invented by Robert Anderson, during almost every decade since there have been attempts at launching commercially viable electric cars. However, the technology did not take center stage until the 2000s. Up till then, the value, risk, and effort equation did not work. Automakers did not go all in on electric vehicles until Tesla paved the way, government incentives and regulations encouraged investment, and infrastructure to extend charging range came to the fore. Finally, the value, risk, and effort required to massively invest in EVs made sense to the auto industry, and Ford, GM, Mercedes, and others shifted resources away from combustion engines only to find consumer interest weak. The value, risk, and effort equation will likely continue to change as the technology evolves.

Chris Yates, former Chief Talent Officer at a major car manufacturer, found himself responsible for guiding a cultural transformation that would allow the company to compete in the EV market. Chris had to find a way to increase the value of the idea while decreasing the risk and the effort. He did so by focusing on the past. "At the company, relationships matter; so did demonstrating you cared about the legacy of the company. I visited plants, worked on shifts, and read the histories. I took our senior leaders to a dinner at the company's museum, and pointed out stories from the twenties, thirties, and forties that laid the groundwork for what we want to do in the EV market. We were not changing our culture; we were going back to our roots." By helping the company rediscover its past, the company could increase the value of their work, while lowering the risk and the effort required to overcome resistance to shifting away from combustion engines.

Once you have identified strengths, weaknesses, and opportunities, consider the threats to the organization. Focus on areas that are external to the organization, threats that could realistically take what is yours—your customers or donors, your revenue, your talent, your business model. While you can focus on existential threats, it is probably more helpful to focus on the threats that have a greater chance of disrupting your organization, like technology or new competitors. In the early 2000s, Target became known for using Red Teams—groups of people dreaming up ways of taking away Target's market share and margins. Then

Target used those sessions to develop tactics for defending their business.

As you consider the threats to your organization, some questions you may ask are:

1. What are the threats to this organization?
2. What technology can disrupt our business?
3. Who is coming for our talent and how will they get them?
4. Who is encroaching on our markets or introducing competing products?
5. What is eroding our revenue or our margins?

Organizations should monitor some threats—for example, if competitors want to buy businesses in your backyard, you should pay attention. Organizations should respond to other threats right away. Companies hire lobbyists all the time to push for legislation they like and to stop legislation they don't. Some threats are fast-moving, like price cuts in the grocery business, and other threats are slow-moving and implacable, like long-term droughts in the Southwestern United States. Both of them impact the price that farmers can charge for their crops, but one impacts the mortgage on your farm today and the other can take away your farm for good.

Assessing what is working and what is not provides leaders with a current-state snapshot of how the organization functions internally and what it competes against externally. Both can have serious implications—for good or ill—on an organization's strategy.

If you want to move beyond a simple SWOT analysis, several

frameworks can help you assess what is working and what is not. For example, Harvard's Michael Porter (2008) developed his five forces model in the late '70s as a way of describing the competitive environment facing organizations. His model examines the power of suppliers and customers, the threat of substitutes, new players in a market, and the rivalry among competitors. Another framework from Harvard, presented in *Blue Ocean Strategy* by Kim and Mauborgne (2005), encourages organizations to find the sweet spot between cost and innovation as a way of creating value for stakeholders. *Blue Ocean Strategy* uses Strategy Canvases as a way of analyzing where competitors invest as they fight over resources and market share. For the visual among us, *Business Model Generation* (Osterwalder & Pigneur, 2010) helps individuals develop business canvases that visually depict business models while helping leaders consider the pains and gains of customers that the organization may address.

### SEEKING FEEDBACK

Feedback is just data. We often attribute emotions like pride or defensiveness to the data we receive from feedback. Our biases shape the feedback we pay attention to or how we use the data to confirm our own conclusions. However, leaders can use feedback as a powerful tool for understanding their performance. Like the gauges in a car, feedback can help leaders determine if the organization is headed in the right direction, going at the right speed, or if there are any warning lights that they need to pay attention to. Again, like conducting a SWOT, in some organizations collecting anything but positive feedback feels risky—as humans we naturally defend, deflect, and deny feedback that does not support our view of the world. As Henry Ford once said, "A customer can have a car painted in any color as long as it is black." He only introduced colors when his competitors sold more cars doing so.

Sources of organizational feedback abound. Talking to key stakeholders is a great way to collect the stories—or the qualitative data—that leaders need to Take Stock of the organization. Board members, employees, customers, key vendors, and suppliers have valuable insights into what is working and what is not. Like Luck Companies, you may discover the truth about your secret sauce or uncover a nugget of wisdom that shifts the focus of your entire strategy. When Charlie Luck came into Luck Stone after his racing career, executives tasked him with running a newly purchased marble quarry in Tennessee. The product had a huge potential market in government buildings, public municipalities, and city halls. Yet the quarry had to produce a consistent color range, which the geology prevented, leaving most of the product as waste. During his tenure running that quarry, Charlie received feedback from customers, plant operators, geologists, and engineers. Data and his own eyes showed him how difficult a challenge the location would prove. In the end, the company could not make the business work and sold it at a loss. As Charlie discovered, using both quantitative and qualitative data is a key step to Taking Stock, in that neither tells the whole story.

Leaders can use customer and employee engagement surveys as another way to collect feedback—which they can aggregate and analyze for trends and relationships between variables. You may see that the leaders with the highest employee engagement scores also have the lowest turnover on their teams, or the customers who return your product did so overwhelmingly because of manufacturing defects. Unfortunately, customers may feel reluctant to fill out feedback surveys if they believe no one is listening or do not believe anyone will take action. Customers may also feel overwhelmed with requests for feedback, especially online. How often are you minding your own business, surfing the web, when a website pop-up asks you to fill out a survey? How often are you waiting on hold for an hour and the company has the gall to ask how they did before they answer the phone? If customers do take the time to provide feedback, they are often upset and screaming into the void, hoping someone will hear them.

Like customers, employees are often skeptical of surveys because they filled them out in the past and nothing happened, or worse, they were singled out and punished for their feedback. Leaders often do a terrible job communicating the results and the actions resulting from such feedback. When seeking feedback, it is important to be honest with ourselves: don't ask questions we don't want the answer to because we might just get it. We ask for feedback, don't like the answers, and do nothing, thereby undermining both our integrity and the integrity of the feedback process.

If you do decide to use surveys to collect feedback, follow a few best practices:

1. Keep them short. Customers, employees, and stakeholders complain about survey fatigue; too many people ask too many questions too often. Keep organizational surveys short, disciplined, and focused.
2. Mix quantitative (think numbers) and qualitative (think stories) questions. Quantitative questions provide metrics you can benchmark, whereas qualitative questions can provide rich examples.

3. If you promise anonymity, you must honor anonymity. If you break someone's trust on this point, you will not receive any more honest feedback.

4. Share your results. To build a Values Based Organization, leaders will need to get comfortable with transparency and honesty about what's working well and what's not. You might not share everything, especially feedback that looks like an outlier or comes across as an unwarranted attack. However, the more you share, the more others will see that you actually want their input, and will be more willing to share it in the future.

5. Take action. Link your actions to the feedback you receive so stakeholders see the connection between their input and your choices, strengthening their willingness to share information in the future.

Keep in mind that how you conduct yourself during this period of Taking Stock will influence how others react the next time you ask for feedback.

More challenging than surveys, but invaluable to your strategy, are focus groups. Not necessarily focus groups led by marketing firms, but leaders talking to real live customers. When Taking Stock, firsthand knowledge proves an invaluable source of data as leaders consider what is working and what is not in an organization. The more senior the executive, the further they are from customers and frontline employees. The feedback funnel becomes a straw, where only tiny bits of information come through, which may or may not be accurate. Some call it the CEO disease. If you're surrounded by people who will only give you positive news or spin feedback so hard it creates a tornado of misleading data, you might just have a case of this disease. Talking to key stakeholders, be they customers or frontline employees, is an excellent use of organizational leadership's time and energy. Surprisingly, leaders do not always make time for these conversations.

When Taking Stock, it is incredibly valuable to find out why someone does not choose us to do business with. If we can make it safe enough for the person to be honest and direct with us, we will often learn incredibly valuable nuggets of wisdom. Maybe they don't like our product, or it doesn't meet their needs. Maybe they don't believe we can provide the value that we promise. Maybe they just don't like us or like someone better. Doing business with others is not just a rational economic exchange—it is often fraught with emotion, feelings, and unconscious assumptions. Looking for the logic might not explain everything.

Part of the feedback challenge is to overcome our natural biases, beliefs, and assumptions to get the data that helps us improve. Politicians ignore polls all the time when the data does not fit their ideology. We often dissuade others from telling us the truth by not asking questions or reacting in a way that shuts down the other person. If you cry every time a customer tells you they prefer a different brand, customers will stop telling you anything. If you want to argue with someone about not choosing your company, you have two choices: A. Be Right or B. Be Happy. Pick one and live with the result.

Getting feedback and the data we need to achieve our goals is one of the most difficult activities Values Based Organizations face. However, by building the curiosity to look in the mirror, to deeply understand what is working and what is not, we can make better choices that align with the organization we want to create and have a stronger impact.

## MEASURING PROGRESS

A cliché that is true in most organizations is the adage "We treasure what we measure" or more darkly, "What gets measured gets managed." I, for one, do not want to be managed; I want to be led. Or more honestly, I want to do the leading. As John Kotter says, "Organizations are overmanaged and underled." However, metrics help us to Take Stock of the organization. They provide feedback and signal if the car is moving in the right direction, at the right speed, with no major issues.

Organizations set goals and establish measures all the time. Many use the SMART approach to setting goals, in that every goal must be Specific, Measurable, Agreed Upon, Realistic, and Time Bound. These SMART goals then have a metric attached to them, such as revenue, growth, or employee engagement.

Metrics have a variety of names: analytics, leading and lagging indicators, grades, etc. The main takeaway is to pick measures that help you understand the outcomes that are important to your business. Accounting drives most of our organizational measures—everything from return on investment or gross margin or cost per widget. Other metrics are unique to the organization, the industry, and the culture. For example, a defense contractor may measure how long it takes to acquire new contracts—speed to approval—while a nonprofit like the YMCA might measure how much money is raised through donations versus revenue generated by memberships. Goodwill stores exist to transform lives through the power of work, so they might measure top-line sales alongside the number of employed associates or even how many people they placed with other organizations. School systems measure graduation rates while publicly traded companies measure their share price.

Key performance indicators, or KPIs, identify the most important sets of data to pay attention to at the organization level. Metrics, on the other hand, may refer to any piece of data that you measure within the organization. For example, the number of steps I take per day might be a metric, while my blood pressure serves as a KPI based on my strategy of not dying. Metrics matter, but KPIs really matter. Choose the critical few that help you measure the health of your organization.

Like all of the Five Practices of Values Based Organizations, Taking Stock is not a one-and-done event. For example, Mitch Haddon, CEO of ColonialWebb, describes "SWOT in the moment," or the ability of his leaders to keep an active SWOT running whenever they make decisions. "Leaders need a little healthy paranoia," says Mitch, and should keep an eye on what's happening in their industries, their markets, with their customers, and their people. Using Taking Stock as a practice—keeping on top of trends and feedback—can help an organization stay nimble and competitive.

**KEY TAKEAWAYS**

To Take Stock we:

- Assess what is working and what is not
- Seek feedback
- Measure progress

# CHAPTER THREE

# Commit to Why and How

Why Commit to Why and How?

Organizations that do not manage their culture are managed by their culture.

Chris Yates has worked at a wide variety of Fortune 500 companies. As a senior leader responsible for culture, Chris has deep experience transforming organizations. "It's not changing the culture," as Chris says, "but rediscovering what's lost." Chris inspires organizations to rediscover the greatness in their history and uses it to support their current strategy. For HSBC, one of the largest banks in the world, it meant remembering that the organization started with the gold of Darius and the Persians, with bankers sailing upriver, holding swords and watching over money boxes. For a major car company, it meant rediscovering the excellence, curiosity, and courage it took to change the world as the company did in the early 1900s yet applied to capturing the EV market today. "It's not about destroying Tesla," says Chris. "Destroying Tesla is just a byproduct of excellence."

At a global technology company, Chris helped lead the cultural shift required to move its products into the cloud while integrating them. "Culture is how you do strategy," says Chris. At this company, according to Chris, "the culture was very aggressive, dog eat dog, and competitive." As a legacy of the founder, the company practiced "precision questioning" where you tested the competence and credibility of others and their ideas by aggressively questioning them, over and over. Precision questioning led to better ideas, but it also led to public humiliation, silos, and an inability to develop partnerships across teams. Without the right culture, the company could not integrate its various product lines to work together as one system.

Chris also served as the Head of Talent at a global heavy equipment manufacturer. At one point in its history, the company did not value safety as it does today. Chris said that in the past "people would die or get burnt or lose limbs." Then at some point, the company took a stand that everyone should go home safe and alive. Culturally, the company leveraged its obsession with quality to obsess about safety. Safety became the number one thing managers reported on. They taught office workers the importance of using handrails in the office, or the safest way to operate a photocopier. At the start of every meeting, they discussed safety. During Chris's time there, when an accident occurred, the entire company of over one hundred thousand employees on six continents would stand down immediately and talk about what happened. That, according to Chris, is the power of culture.

Why does why matter? Human beings are meaning-making machines. We hunger to know that our actions matter. We want to contribute to something larger than ourselves. Research backs this up. For example, when study participants report that they have a strong sense of meaning in their lives, they report positive life outcomes like less heart disease, less Alzheimer's risk, and less feelings of burnout and stress. The opposite is also true: having the sense that one's work does not matter and feeling no sense of individual purpose in an organization leads to feelings of social isolation and antisocial behaviors, and it may contribute to self-harm. For Guy Clumper, President of Holt Development, the business reason for Why is simple: "When people feel like they matter, they make other people feel like they matter."

Meaningful work also matters. Those with a stronger sense of meaning at work have higher performance, are less likely to leave, and display higher levels of commitment to the organization. The downside is most employees—researchers disagree on the exact percentage—experience little sense of meaning in their work lives. They work for a paycheck. Some employers feel comfortable with this mentality—they want warm bodies that they can replace at a moment's notice to fill a role, not real living breathing humans who can contribute more than the bare minimum if you ask and inspire them.

On the surface, most jobs seem as if they are designed to sap any sort of meaning from our lives. And yet, with a little bit of why, construction jobs become jobs that house people, line jobs in manufacturing plants become jobs that provide people with clothing that brings them joy, and sales jobs become problem-solving machines for customers. Jobs have meaning if we infuse them with meaning; jobs can be lifeless if we drain the joy from them like some sort of meaning-sucking vampires. If you are a formal leader in an organization, you have a choice—so choose not to be a vampire. "Human beings have a capacity to focus on scarcity or abundance," says Guy. Leaders can infuse jobs with either fear of loss or a sense of possibility. "When you lead with scarcity, you're fighting an uphill battle. When you lead with abundance, you have a chance because we have enough challenges as it is."

By Committing to Why and How, organizations take the time to define why the organization exists—its mission, and how the work gets done—its values. This happens by doing these three things:

- Refine our mission
- Operationalize our values
- Clarify expectations

"Culture" feels like a squishy word to describe a very real phenomenon of organizations. Culture is the shared values, beliefs, and assumptions that drive behaviors and decision-making in organizations. It emerges as people interact—put two people in a room, tell them they are in business together, and five minutes later you will have a culture.

Culture matters because it impacts everything that happens in an organization: How is the service? Culture. Who gets promoted? Culture. How is conflict managed? Culture. It even influences processes like pricing. Has anyone ever said to you, "We can't raise prices, customers might leave!" Culture. Or, "We will raise prices; those customers have no choice!" Culture. Culture can drive everything from where you put your company headquarters to how many pages are in your company handbook. Don't believe me? Check out Tesla's handbook leaked online a few years ago. It is four pages long and includes the line "If you don't call or don't show up for work you are a jerk." (*Tesla Anti Handbook*, pg. 3). It also outlines the "stupid stuff" you shouldn't do, like steal or do drugs on company property. Overall, Tesla's handbook is four pages long, doesn't take itself too seriously, and describes employees as adults who have common sense. Culture.

Now if you've ever managed people, you have learned that not everybody has common sense. And sometimes our workplaces perform like adult daycares—the kids run wild, someone needs a change, everyone could use a nap, and you want to pull your hair out. Ford's code of conduct, for example, has over sixty pages and explicitly describes what to do about gifts, favors, international operations, bribes, intellectual property, and everything else you can think of. Ford's handbook clearly states what the company tolerates and what it does not, and it references the Office of the General Counsel—their lawyers—a lot. Ford's handbook is a serious document for serious people. Culture.

Tesla and Ford compete in the marketplace for your dollars and pursue different strategies for doing so. Their cultures influence their strategies. While these companies can choose a strategy that does not fit their culture, they do so at their peril...as Peter Drucker is rumored to have said, "Culture eats strategy for breakfast." An operationally efficient culture built around few defects, high output, and low margins will struggle with innovation. A culture that rewards individual performance will struggle with teamwork. A culture that detests rules will reject any kind of formalization. In the EV market, if Ford destroys Tesla, it is a by-product of Ford's culture.

Some organizational cultures are consistent throughout the organization, some are made up of subcultures that may have a tenuous connection to one another, and some may be very fragmented because of company size or geography. For example, Chik-fil-A, a chain of restaurants rapidly expanding throughout the United States, keeps its culture aligned through a variety of tools, including training and assiduously choosing who franchises its restaurants. No matter what Chik-fil-A restaurant you visit, you will hear "My pleasure" after you interact with employees. Visit a McDonalds in San Diego and then one in New York, and you will likely have a completely different experience.

Industry or the type of organization can also influence culture. According to John Pullen, Chief Growth Officer of Luck Companies, "In the construction industry, I see a strong bias for an internal focus on operational excellence, because that's the way you sustain the business." In startup companies, experimentation and innovation are key. Meagan Metzger, founder of a startup called Dcode based in Washington, DC, has a process she describes as "Keep, kill, double down, or modify." New ideas get a trial run, and if they don't perform the company kills the idea and moves on.

Regulations, lawsuits, and the nature of how organizations generate revenue can also influence culture. A well-known tobacco company suffered through a major lawsuit, which according to insiders stifled its ability to innovate for years by encouraging a culture of fear.

People influence culture, then the culture influences people. For example, at Dcode, Meagan's core values influenced the culture of the organization. "I was an athlete," says Meagan, "so I wanted a workplace where people worked together as a team. Teamwork would anchor me for the day, or I would be shouting at people to pump them up." As the company grew, added more staff, and eventually developed more processes and procedures, the fun began to leak out of the organization and Meagan. "My gut was screaming at me, but I didn't listen," she says. Eventually, she began to reinject the practices that she felt reinforced her hunger for teams, energy, and joy while getting a lot accomplished. "People aren't here just for the money. And I want them to want to come to work."

In family businesses, the family's values often influence the culture of the business. At Luck Companies, the founder of the company, Charles S. Luck Jr., cared about his people, cooking for them in a specially made train car. His values influenced his son, who took up the mantra of "We Care." The founder's grandson Charlie has led the company with a mission of Igniting Human Potential. No doubt Charlie's son Richard will continue the family's legacy of focusing on people. The culture we create in our organizations can have a multigenerational impact, influencing parents to children, and children to grandchildren. Despite being publicly traded, at 120 years old, Ford runs like a family business, according to insiders. On the other hand, Bill Gates's habit of challenging ideas and people has influenced generations of Microsoft employees.

In every organization, senior leaders influence the organization's culture because they control the tools that move a culture: power, policy, process, money, and structure. They also influence culture because they model behaviors and make decisions based on their own beliefs and assumptions. With time and repetition, these decisions get embedded within the culture of the organization. Employees learn to think like their bosses, and begin to unconsciously ask "WWTBD"...What would the boss do? The boss, in turn, gets influenced by the culture they lead, resulting in a self-reinforcing feedback loop.

As such an intrinsic part of organizations, culture influences the company's secret sauce, or why it is successful. Tesla, focused on developing a meritocracy of independent thinkers, has created a culture where employees challenge the old-school rules of car building, leading to a wide range of innovations. On the other hand, sometimes the cars' panels fall off. Academics have described culture as a resource that employees use to serve customers or each other.

Culture, however, can be tricky. If you don't manage your culture, it will manage you. While cultures arise from the complex systems of organizations, cultures resist being controlled but can be influenced. We designed each of the Five Practices of Values Based Organizations to influence culture, most directly by refining the organization's mission, operationalizing its values, and clarifying expectations.

### REFINING OUR MISSION

Luck Companies' original mission had deep roots in its history in operations—the company's why focused on being a family-held, multistate, construction aggregates and materials supplier. The mission lacked joy and a sense of purpose but felt directionally correct to employees. But then 2008 happened. Over the course of six months, 60 percent of Luck's business evaporated, and over eighteen months, leaders reduced the company by half. Like most companies in the construction business, Luck struggled to keep the lights on after the highs of the early 2000s. At the same time as the global economic meltdown, Charlie Luck grew ill, while his sister and mother both developed cancer. Charlie went through a crisis of body, mind, and soul. He nearly died, confined to his bed for sixteen hours out of a twenty-four-hour day for weeks.

During that time Charlie considered the big questions that frenzied workweeks, heavy responsibilities, and jammed calendars prevented: "Why did this happen to me? What will I do if I survive? Why does the company exist?" When he finally returned to work months later, the company had stabilized. Given his bedridden experience, Charlie announced that the company would stand for more than just making money. He wanted to make a positive difference in the world. He wasn't sure how but knew the company should. Other than simply making small rocks out of big rocks, the company had core competencies in leadership and culture. Company leaders decided to take what they knew about both into the world. Luck's mission—its why—became Igniting Human Potential. Luck is no longer just in the business of crushing rocks; it is also in the people business. And that has made all the difference.

Luck Companies' mission helps the company describe why it exists and the impact it wants to make. Luck wants people to reach their potential—whether they are chasing their wildest dreams or becoming the best parent they can be. Whatever they choose, the company wants them to meet and exceed their own expectations of who they are and what they are capable of. Those associates will make a positive difference in the lives of the people they work with, their customers and vendors, their families and communities. Luck's leadership believes ignited people are more engaged, leading to higher levels of service, innovation, and performance. These lead to higher profitability and revenues, which the company reinvests in its people. By doing good, the company does well. The mission gives the company an overarching reason to do everything they do, knowing that the work will last decades and will impact multiple generations. Different authors define organizational missions and visions in different ways. There is no singular definition for either. For our purposes, "mission" describes an organization's why—why it exists, what purpose it serves, and what impact it wants to make. "Vision" describes what an organization wants to accomplish over time. Missions tend to last for years or even decades, while visions set what Collins and Porras described in *Built to Last* as a BHAG: a big, hairy, audacious goal.

Much like individuals who have a personal why that guides their lives, organizations have a mission that guides decisions over the course of multiple strategic planning windows. For example, an organization's why might be to provide jobs for a community or to produce innovations that save lives. If it's a family business, its mission might be to provide generational wealth for the founder's descendants. If it is a nonprofit, the organization's mission defines what public good it serves. A few examples of missions include:

- Dcode: Making the Government Better Through Technology
- Luck Companies: Igniting Human Potential
- Goodwill: Transforming Lives through the Power of Work

Visions, on the other hand, serve as the overarching goal for one strategic plan. Using Goodwill for example, while the organization's mission is to transform lives through the power of work, the vision for a local Goodwill chapter may be to provide jobs for two thousand people who have barriers to employment such as disabilities or poverty. For Dcode, the mission is to make the government better, but the company's vision is to triple in size in three years.

To influence culture, refining an organization's mission should answer the question of "Why do we exist?" While likely implicit in the organization, until we clarify the words and put pen to paper, employees may not act on it. Once written down, leaders can use the mission to provide clarity for employees, customers, clients, and vendors alike. While missions may seem obvious—"our company exists to make money" or "our organization exists to serve clients" or "our business exists to keep Grandpa out of Grandma's hair"—refining a mission provides the opportunity to strengthen alignment across the organization.

In order to refine an organization's mission, leaders should ask a series of questions such as:

- Why do we exist?
- What impact do we want to make?
- What is our purpose?

We describe the action as "refining our mission" because many organizations already have mission statements. They tend to be long, filled with what my grandmother would call "five-dollar words," and disconnected from the real work of the organization. Developed at a retreat years ago by completely different leaders, those mission statements hold little emotional connection to today's leaders. Refining is not always about starting from scratch, but about taking what is still relevant and building on it.

### OPERATIONALIZING OUR VALUES

Over eight years ago, Meagan Metzger, founder and CEO of Dcode, emailed five hundred venture capitalists to say, "We can make the federal market easy for tech companies." She did not have a company. She did not have a solution. But she saw a gap in the market and knew she could fill it. "It was a build-the-plane-as-you-fly kind of move," she says. Eight years later, Dcode's mission is all about making the government better by teaching the government how to work with tech, and tech how to work with the government.

Meagan instinctively understood the kind of company she wanted to build. "The day I hired my first employee, we sat down in a bar in San Francisco, and I said, "We need to decide right now what kind of culture and company we want." Meagan knew she wanted to build a team that worked hard and played hard, where no one was above doing any job. "We call it 'No Dcoder left behind,'" she says. "People shouldn't be on an island working their butts off without their team to help them out." Early on she set the tone for having fun and getting pumped up for work, through silly hats, a celebratory Slack channel called Dunk Hard, and everyone identifying their Dcode Hug.

Creating alignment throughout Dcode, from its culture to its strategy, plays an important role in the organization. "I think if people are rowing their boat in the same direction, and if they know people have their backs, you get a lot more done," Meagan says. Goals, accountability, and fun drive the company. "Not everyone is going to be your A+ player," she says, and you need to "wash them out of the system" if they don't aspire to high performance. Meagan believes you shouldn't leave any of your expectations a mystery, whether they are your goals, your cultural expectations, or your feedback. "We talk about what we are good at, what we are bad at, how well we define things, and whether or not we are on the same page. Our delivery teams are so mission obsessed," says Meagan, "if there's work we are doing that is not aligned with our mission of making the government better, we have to talk about it."

Alignment means making difficult choices as well. "We had a double-digit millions opportunity that we just walked away from. We recognized that our potential partner did not value the same things. If we were just obsessed with our own growth goals, we would have taken the deal. But we connected it back to our culture and values and killed the deal. You have to make some decisions that make sure people are on the same page."

As the leader of the organization, Meagan recognizes that if she wants others to follow her vision, she has to share it again and again. "You need to help others be bought in and sold on the idea, to see how their work is contributing and that they believe what you are doing is worthwhile." Another approach she has instilled in the organization is the idea of adding value. In every interaction with clients, they aim to add value and make it worth others' time. "You sell or deliver things differently when you are constantly thinking about your stakeholders and what's in it for them."

Every organization has values, most have values listed on their website, and some even describe the culture of the organization. The classic example of values from the 1990s and early 2000s were Enron's: integrity, communication, respect, and excellence. Enron imploded after investors discovered that for years, the company booked revenue it had not earned, inflating its profits and stock price before going bankrupt in 2001. Having organizational values on a website does not make an organization a Values Based Organization—however, defining those values, communicating them effectively and often throughout the organization, and using those values to make decisions does. Most organizations stop well short of any of these activities. But values, when defined, communicated, integrated into processes, and driven throughout an organization provide a powerful tool for managing culture.

Values have a long history—followers expected pharaohs in ancient Egypt to rule with and be ruled by truth, justice, and righteousness. Confucian ideals of integrity, knowledge, and benevolence spread through ancient China. Socrates taught his students about the cultivation of virtue. The Ten Commandments implored Jews and later Christians to live lives of piety and faith. Examples abound of leaders, religions, and teachers imparting values to their people. In the late eighteenth century, as industrialization transformed the nature of work, the need to guide organizational decisions and behaviors arose, and with it the idea of guiding values. Later, in the 1970s and '80s, organizational theorists and consultants like Peter Drucker, Peters & Waterman, Edgar Schein, and Kouzes & Posner focused less on the technical aspects of optimizing companies and more on the human aspects of performance.

Operationalizing Our Values means describing the culture you want to create in the organization, and then using values as a way of defining the culture. For example, at Luck Companies, "integrity" means "earning the trust and respect of others." Additionally, leaders should provide more clarity about what the values look like in action by identifying behaviors that support the values. For example, at Luck, "integrity" includes "being honest" and "holding self and others accountable." At Mitchells, a family-owned luxury retailer, the values include data, customers, excellence, and relationships. As an operationalized value, "data" means "information-based decision-making" and includes the behaviors of "using technology to stay personal" and "knowing the score." As a retailer whose mission is to "Make people feel great!," the value of data underlines how important running a smart business is alongside building relationships with customers.

When most organizations define their values, and therefore their culture, they neglect the usability of their values statements. If you operationalize your values, it means you are going to use them. Actively. Every day. To drive decisions. Which means everyone in the organization must understand them. Again, you want to avoid my grandmother's "five-dollar words."

Some organizations never clearly define their values. One person may describe "innovation" as "ideas that add value" while another person may describe "innovation" as "developing creative ideas." While both are perfectly valid, they will drive different behaviors when put into practice. If we simply tell our employees to be innovative, they won't have the slightest clue if that means changing out the chips in the snack machines for pretzels, or if it means fundamentally rethinking our entire business strategy. But hey, be innovative!

Other organizations define their values so densely, and so completely, that they become overburdened by words and have very little chance of being used. It is as if organizations don't really want employees to think for themselves or maybe they have been sued over what seemed like common sense at the time. Either way, employees will tuck that hundred-page manifesto on a shelf, never to be read or heard from again, at least until the next consultant comes by to lead a values exercise.

At Luck Companies, the organization went through a period where it had organizational values, brand behaviors, and competing customer value propositions. By themselves, these ideas were fine, but all together created a mess for associates who had to navigate what they should focus on and when. On top of this confusion, the organization chose words that did not resonate with the mainly blue-collar population. For example, one of the values behaviors was "embrace ambiguity." Most associates did not know what "ambiguity" meant in a one-hundred-year-old stone company, much less how to use it in casual conversation: "I smelled ambiguity this morning and felt perturbed." Mentors of mine like Jay Coffman and Guy Clumpner like to say, "Words matter." And they do, especially when using values as a tool for guiding culture. It took time, but eventually, the company settled on "be open to change" instead of "embrace ambiguity."

When it comes to operationalizing values, follow the steps below originally inspired by Blanchard and O'Connor's book *Managing By Values* (2003):

1.  Consider the strengths and weaknesses of the current culture. What's working? What's not?
2.  Consider the culture of the future. What needs to be transformed or added?
3.  Identify what values capture the strengths of the past and the needs for the future. And keep the list short. Four is plenty. Eighteen is overkill.
4.  Define your four values. What do they mean in action? We are using values to drive behaviors and decision-making, so all of your values statements should have a bias for action. Think verbs.
5.  Identify what behaviors support each of the values. Again, keep it simple. Use words your organization uses. If they don't use five-dollar words, don't use five-dollar words to define your values. Remember that you want everyone in the organization to understand these behaviors and act on them. Consider your frontline employee, whether they drive a forklift, use a cash register, or conduct experiments in a lab. If your frontline scientist/cashier/forklift operator can't understand them, keep refining the behaviors until they can.

If you follow these best practices, your values will look something like the integrity value of Luck Companies:

INTEGRITY

Earn the trust and respect of others.

- Be honest.
- Do what you say.
- Hold self and others accountable.

- Give and receive feedback.

Or the data value of Mitchells:

## DATA

Information-based decision-making.

- Know the score.
- Use technology to stay personal.
- Ensure the financial success of the business.
- Hold self and others accountable.

Operationalizing Your Values is a process that does more than just describe the culture you want to create. If done well, it can be a powerful tool for influencing others. In some companies, the CEO goes off in the woods, howls at the moon, and emerges with a set of values the next morning, and it does nothing to move the culture. A better process includes senior leaders, who will need to lead around the culture you want to create. An even better process would be to develop a rough draft of values, definitions, and behaviors with the senior-most leaders and ask key influencers for feedback.

The goal of this process is to help people understand the culture you want to create and why, describe what their values look like in action, and have some ownership in the final product. Ultimately, getting feedback will also help you avoid the curse of five-dollar words guaranteed to irritate your employees. Every culture has trigger words that will absolutely earn mockery and disdain if not avoided—like "ambiguity" at Luck Companies. Another example the company faced involved having a strong safety culture yet using the phrase "take appropriate risks" as part of the values definitions. The phrase made no sense to employees who thought risks, even appropriate ones, were bad. Involving more employees than just senior leaders will help you avoid pitfalls such as these. As you consider who to involve, try and balance efficiency and speed with buy-in and acceptance. Involving others in the conversation is the first step to influencing them to act on your values.

## CLARIFY EXPECTATIONS

Cultures celebrate some behaviors and condemn others. I've seen strong sales cultures where the outside sales force operated like lone cowboys, who were rewarded for getting the sale no matter the hurdle, no matter the pressures that sale put on operations or other teams. I've seen startup cultures that were allergic to process and discipline, that pinballed from idea to idea in a way that prevented them from ever scaling. I've seen engineering cultures so focused on technical specifications that they often missed what customers actually wanted. None of these behaviors are good or bad by themselves—but the context and the strategy of the organization make them so. A startup that wants to scale must develop process and discipline. An engineering firm that wants to grow must listen to clients. The culture that encourages these behaviors in support of the organization's goals can provide clarity and reinforcement in a way that moves beyond simple carrots and sticks (or rewards and consequences).

One of the goals of Values Based Organizations is to inspire commitment and not just compliance. Compliant employees give you the bare minimum effort, while committed employees give you that extra push that takes a mediocre customer experience and makes it dazzle. Often, leaders use rewards and discipline to reinforce compliance—do this or else. Without a strong why or how, rewards and discipline drive short-term behaviors, since employees want to get paid and don't want to get fired. However, their motivation tends not to last.

The final two practices of Values Based Organizations, Championing Values Based Leadership and Engaging Everyone, help build commitment across organizations, but that commitment starts with clarifying expectations based on the culture the organization wants to create—i.e., newly operationalized values.

To clarify expectations, leaders will need to communicate the values, definitions, and behaviors throughout the organization. Like any change in management process, the organization will go through a learning curve on its way to becoming a Values Based Organization.

THE STEPS OF LEARNING

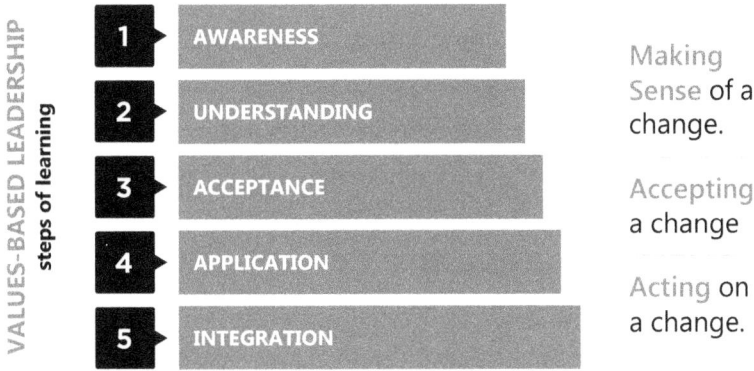

VALUES-BASED LEADERSHIP
steps of learning

| 1 | AWARENESS | Making Sense of a change. |
| 2 | UNDERSTANDING | |
| 3 | ACCEPTANCE | Accepting a change |
| 4 | APPLICATION | Acting on a change. |
| 5 | INTEGRATION | |

||| INNERWILL

At the beginning of a change, such as implementing new values, the first step in the Steps of Learning is Awareness. It means that you have made employees aware that a change is coming. It does not mean that they agree or are excited or even really know what you are talking about.

As you continue your efforts to lead around such a change, your goal is to get employees to Understanding. Meaning they understand its scope, what you are asking of them, and how it will impact both them and the organization. It means they have made sense of the change, but it does not mean they feel good or bad about it. Often leaders spend so much time living with a change and planning on its perfect execution that they forget what it is like to be unaware of it. Then when they throw a big party to announce the change, they get upset that employees don't feel as excited as they do or that they can't see the vision. Employees can't feel committed to the change because they haven't had time to make sense of it yet.

When Scott Evans and Kristin Ogo, the CEO and COO of Kenmore Envelope, first approached their adjusters with a vision of outservicing their competitors to win more customers, the operators balked. They did not see Scott's vision or believe they could run their plant as flexibly as Kristin demanded. "It's black and white," they said, "we can't do that." Scott and Kristin had to move their employees from Awareness to Understanding, building a client-focused mindset.

The third step of any change initiative is Acceptance. Acceptance means that employees metaphorically nod their heads yes and agree to make changes, not because they must but because they want to. In many change efforts, organizations never get to Acceptance. Only time and turnover lead to a grudging acknowledgment that things are different. When building a Values Based Organization, earning acceptance is crucial, especially with the senior-most leaders and the key influencers. If you don't have acceptance at the top of the organization, or if you neglect to get the acceptance of the gatekeepers that everyone looks to, you won't ever get the whole organization to change. However, if you get the senior leaders and the key influencers, you get everybody.

In Kenmore, Scott and Kristin had to get the acceptance and buy-in of their floor supervisors first, then the senior adjusters that everyone looked to. Slowly, over time, they built the company's capacity to produce more complicated envelopes, at faster speeds, and with higher quality. "We didn't lose efficiency," says Kristin, "but we put pressure on the operation to produce more work." Not through carrots and sticks, but by leading with their service vision, building teams, and leveling up their skills. As Scott likes to say, "Speed wins."

Some part of me wishes that change management occurs in organizations from the bottom up, but in my twenty-five years of doing this work across hundreds of organizations, I have never experienced change succeed without starting at the senior-most levels of an organization. As complex systems, you never have complete control over what happens within organizations, as chance, competing forces, unexpected consequences, and imperfect social networks influence the speed and adoption of any change, much in the same way a pinball bounces around a machine. Sometimes you pull the plunger, bang the bumpers, and hope for the best. While the results feel unpredictable, leaders can influence their organization's culture with effort and time. Scott and Kristin could have hoped that the culture would change on its own; instead, they made a conscious effort to help their employees accept the change. The time required depends on the organization and how much senior leaders invest in making changes. In my experience, with a year to eighteen months' worth of investment, leaders can make significant changes within their organizations. At Kenmore, the culture has evolved over a number of years, starting with Scott's entrance into the business and continuing to this day.

The fourth step of any change is Application, or employees trying new behaviors, experimenting with new processes, or simply doing something different. With enough choices that align with the new values and behaviors, the culture begins to change first on teams, then departments, business units, and organizations. At Kenmore, adjusters running the envelope folding machines began to compete against their own production metrics, pushing the machinery past what they once thought impossible. Shifts began to work together more closely instead of blaming each other for shortcomings. Sales and operations communicated more regularly. Customers noticed and brought the company more complicated work and more revenue. As more employees reached Application and tried more things, the more the overall culture started to evolve. Today, Kenmore has reached Integration, where the changes started by Kristin and Scott years ago seem like a fact of organizational life and not something new and tenuous. The company's new values—reputation, passion, community, drive, and safety—have become the way it has always been.

To move employees through the Steps of Learning, leaders must clarify expectations along each step of the way. At the Awareness stage, leaders communicate that they want to transform the culture, introducing new values, and new expectations for the organization to put those values into action. At this stage, leaders should focus on what will change and why. Like a bell curve, on the right of the curve, some employees will feel excited, on the left of the curve some will feel unhappy, and in the middle others will feel neutral. At the Understanding step, leaders introduce specifics about the new values and behaviors and provide more clarity about how the organization will use those values to make decisions. Leaders will often use storytelling to help employees understand how to apply new behaviors to their specific roles.

The Understanding step can take quite some time as employees try to make sense of the values and may only grasp at a surface level what is required of them to use values to make decisions. For example, when Kenmore implemented their value of drive, they defined it as a fire in the belly to succeed. The behaviors included winning together, taking personal accountability, staying hungry, and that speed wins. Kristin and Scott set the expectation that when recruiting new employees, managers needed to look for candidates who wanted to win as a team, who were hungry to keep learning and keep going, and who were comfortable going fast. At the Understanding step, leaders should engage employees in lengthy conversations about their own ideas for implementing the values in the organization, what the obstacles may be, and with as little judgment as possible, how the employees feel about the change. Writing new expectations in a policy handbook is not enough—employees need the chance to process the information, either on their own or in groups, through reflection on their own and out loud in conversation. Only when they make sense of the new values and agree with the benefits of the transformed culture will they reach Acceptance. Kristin, Scott, and the rest of their leadership team spent months at this step, slowly building employee understanding of their vision for the future of the organization.

Application as a step may take longer than Understanding, as employees need a chance to practice new behaviors. At Luck Companies, it became clear that the company had to build a core competency of giving and getting feedback. In the beginning, associates struggled with how to deliver feedback that the other person could hear and act upon. Associates also struggled to get the feedback they needed to improve, moving beyond their own biases or competing commitments. Although now feedback forms an essential part of the organization's culture, driven by the company values of integrity and leadership, it took years to fully integrate feedback into the culture.

Ultimately, clarifying expectations requires leaders to communicate how the organization will implement its operationalized values, then leading around those values through each stage of the Steps of Learning. Clarifying expectations means taking the idea of values and catalyzing it throughout an organization, building the organization's Commitment to Why and How.

**KEY TAKEAWAYS**

To Commit to Why and How we:

- Refine our mission
- Operationalize our values
- Clarify expectations

# CHAPTER FOUR

# Align Action, Part 1

Why does Aligning Action matter?

Organizations without a plan for how to create the future waste their time, energy, and resources due to a lack of focus.

John Pullen, the Chief Growth Officer of Luck Companies, faced a dilemma. The company had just survived the worst construction downturn in its history, and he had just been named Luck Stone's new President. The company's strategy until that time meant becoming even better operators, and John knew that the company would need a different approach to growth. "The company had a long history of being focused on operational excellence," says John, "but you need to balance that against profoundly understanding your customers and markets." John told his new executive team, "Let's make this strategy about customers, understanding our markets, and innovation. Let's go ask our customers what they believe about the company." As the team made progress, it encountered the dynamics of the company's operations culture. The team wondered, "Why do we need to make the customer a priority? Our sales guys don't sell, they just take quotes. We just need to produce as efficiently as possible." In those conversations, John discovered firsthand the power of culture to impact strategy, and how crucial changing the mindsets of senior leaders would prove. For John, any successful strategy includes three factors:

**Factor One:** "If you're going to think about the strategic direction of the company, you always want to tie it to the culture and mission of the business. It's a must." He used this lesson when approaching a new growth strategy for the business. "The first question we wrestled with when it came to growth was the connection back to our values and mission." The Values Based culture of the company and the mission of Igniting Human Potential meant that the company had to think about how any decision impacted people. "We had a lot of talent and emerging leaders in the business," says John, "and if we didn't provide them a runway, we were going to lose people. How do we grow and sustain our talent?" The second values and mission question John led the organization to wrestle with focused on the positive impact the company could make in new and different communities. "We asked, 'How do we activate the mission of the company while building a financially sustainable model?'"

**Factor Two:** "If you develop a strategy and initiate it, you better make sure that you've got the right cultural mindset of why you're doing it before you blast it out into the world. It's a calculus for disaster." For example, the biggest mistake many companies make is building assets before they build mindset. "It's one of the most risky constructs you can have in business," says John. Luck faced this problem in its architectural stone business. "We moved from a contractor-centered view to a designer/customer-centered view that was a massive mindset change for all of our associates, customers, and vendors. We built very high-end design centers, but many of the associates didn't understand the value proposition and struggled to execute on the strategy. The customers' experience, the culture, and the mindset never really aligned." Several years later, the company sold off its architectural stone business amid a deep housing recession and poor results from the strategic reset.

With this lesson in mind, as the company embarked on geographically growing its aggregate division, John first had to build support at the top of the business. John started by sharing stories about the company's associates, and why it risked losing phenomenally talented people. He shared data about growth in the company's current footprint and markets, pointing out that "if we wanted to sustain a successful, multigenerational, multidecade company," the company had to move with population growth. He asked questions that focused leadership on external factors: What was going on in public infrastructure? Where was the industry going? What are our customers saying? What companies were for sale? What opportunities were there for growth? John's goals included building a passion for growth and geographic expansion at the top of the business.

John then had to change the mindset of the directors and senior managers of the business because "they have to receive the vision but also execute on the work." To drive execution, "they have to believe in what you are doing, have clarity about what you're doing, and they have to be vision inspired by the right leaders to push that work forward with momentum. When that group picks the ball up and runs with it, then you actually see some things happen."

Finally, John had to influence the mindsets of the frontline associates to help them recognize the role they play in the company's growth. He went out into the field, visiting each location, and sharing the company's growth strategy at a high level, getting them to think about their role in the organization's strategy. He told them, "When you walk into a Luck Stone operation, and you see how amazing this place runs, how efficient and safe it is, the level of care and focus we put on aesthetics, and how we treat our communities, you give me the credibility to talk about growth in the company because of how you run the company."

**Factor Three:** "You've got to align all the parts of your enterprise—like a portfolio." Shared services like Human Resources or Information Technology, different operating units, any real estate you own—should all be aligned. "You have to align it vertically and horizontally," to make sure the different parts of the enterprise catalyze each other. Along with other senior leaders, John worked closely with the CFO to help the company reorganize how its capital structure and assets supported the broader strategy of growth. Alignment at this level of the business can open up opportunities for adjacent revenue streams, products, and opportunities that otherwise would not exist. At the same time, according to John, a new strategy can't imbalance the company by putting too many resources into a new strategy and neglecting the core business and heritage markets. In Luck's case, the heritage locations needed to remain well-resourced and sustained.

All the work the company has done to create alignment, change mindsets, and manage the portfolio of the business has a long-term impact. "It's going to lead us to another step function in revenue growth, geographic expansion, and excellence in different areas. It's going to be better than it's ever been."

In the 1970s and '80s, strategy set the world of management on fire. Strategy this, strategy that, all we need is a strategy to win. Strategies such as Honda's efforts to destroy Yamaha's motorcycles, American car manufacturers competing with Japanese imports through new lines like Saturn, offshoring to cut costs then onshoring when global supply chains faltered, all had their roots in this movement. But strategy—a plan to realize a mission and achieve a vision—is never enough. Strategies require the aligned actions of leaders and employees, along with the will and the skill to achieve them.

Aligned Action should result from any worthwhile strategic planning process. The process means more than just producing a business plan, it serves to get everyone on the same page (rowing in the same direction, marching up the same hill, singing from the same songbook—choose your metaphor). Aligning Action is about influence—how can we get employees to act in support of shared goals, driven by commitment, not compliance?

The Aligning Action process includes three steps:

- Evolving our vision and strategy
- Strengthening relationships
- Improving core processes

This chapter focuses on the first step of Aligning Action, evolving our vision and strategy.

As a reminder, for our purposes, we will use the following definitions:

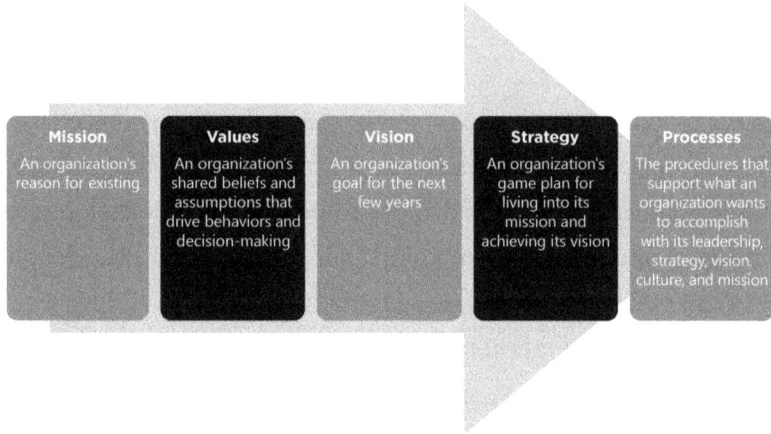

| Mission | Values | Vision | Strategy | Processes |
|---------|--------|--------|----------|-----------|
| An organization's reason for existing | An organization's shared beliefs and assumptions that drive behaviors and decision-making | An organization's goal for the next few years | An organization's game plan for living into its mission and achieving its vision | The procedures that support what an organization wants to accomplish with its leadership, strategy, vision, culture, and mission |

You may have seen these terms defined differently by different authors in different books, especially "mission" and "vision." We will be consistent throughout this book using these terms and these definitions for clarity, because as Brené Brown says in her book *Daring Greatly*, "Clarity is kind."

## EVOLVING OUR VISION AND STRATEGY

Vision, a Big Hairy Audacious Goal for the future, gives us a North Star to journey toward. It lights the way and provides inspiration for employees. Vision is about seeing into the future, while strategy is about charting a course to get there successfully. Some believe that visions are not meant to be achieved but are purely aspirational and inspirational. I don't believe that in the least.

Why set a goal you can't achieve? That way results in madness and frustration. Pick something you can reasonably do, that stretches you over the next few years, challenges your people, and breathes life into the organization. (Don't forget that "inspiration" is based on the Latin word *inspiratus*, to breathe into). "Yamaha wo tsubusu!" "We will crush Yamaha!" probably inspired Honda to evolve as a business, offer multiple new models, and slash prices, stealing away Yamaha's market share and profitability. "Destroy Tesla" does not have the same ring to it, but as a vision for the big three American car makers, it will likely breathe lots of inspiration into these companies.

As one of the practices of Values Based Organizations, Aligning Action requires decisions at every level of the organization to support what the organization wants to achieve with its mission and vision. By evolving the vision and strategy, the organization could adjust its course to the prevailing winds of the marketplace. Strategy should not appear as set in stone but should evolve organically as the world evolves. Strategy requires the paradox of maintaining a big goal and plan for getting there while adapting that plan if the world tilts on its axis, like during the early onset of COVID-19.

Setting a vision is inextricable from developing strategy—I will often work with organizations to develop them simultaneously. Vision and strategy do not need to drastically depart from the current successes of the organization—most strategic plans evolve incrementally. Sometimes, however, organizations must evolve or die. Bankruptcy is not just an idea, it is a thing that happens to companies every day, leaving them in the dustbin of history (Enron, Blockbuster) or alive in a much-reduced way (Circuit

City, Kodak). More recent examples, like Bed Bath and Beyond's overwhelming debt and inability to adapt illustrate how much vision and strategy matter, just as WeWork's fall stemmed from a lack of solid business fundamentals.

There is a strong argument for incremental change in business strategy; the best strategies work when everyone understands them inside and outside of the organization—including customers, suppliers, employees, the board, and stakeholders. That clarity takes time to build. Secondly, the best strategies have distilled the organization's secret sauce into everything they do, which also takes time. If the organization's customers and stakeholders value that secret sauce, the organization should deliver that sauce again and again. This requires quite a bit of "value chain optimizing"—or more simply, tweaking how you execute on your business until you get really good at it. To do so requires leaders to build an operation that consistently delivers on their secret sauce—or, in MBA speak, to develop an operationally efficient enterprise whose value chain consistently delivers on its customer value proposition. Be really good at what your customers want to pay for. That's a great business strategy.

Challenges sometimes require organizations to drastically change their strategies—new entrants threaten your existing customers, market forces threaten to capsize your industry, or new technologies rapidly supplant existing ones. Widespread, GPS-capable cell phones enabled Uber to disrupt the taxi marketplace, putting a lot of traditional companies out of business. Netflix figuring out how to keep people on their couches and not in video stores killed Blockbuster. Drastic change for change's sake is a disaster, but organizations should spend time scanning the environment, trying to understand where the puck—or the economy—is going. Then they can adjust their strategy to fit their prediction of the future.

Strategic planning, whether incremental or revolutionary, follows the same steps with a few key differences.

## BASIC STEPS IN STRATEGIC PLANNING

In the following pages, we will cover the ten steps in basic strategic planning:

1. Make the case for why.
2. Get the right people in the room.
3. Get the right data.
4. Conduct a SWOT analysis.
5. Challenge your assumptions.
6. Bucket your conclusions.
7. Determine your vision.
8. Determine what success looks like.
9. Develop tactics and a budget.
10. Establish an organizational rhythm.

### 1. Make the case for why.

If your organization has a long history of strategic planning, and everyone has bought into the process, feel free to skip this step. For many organizations, however, you need to make a case for why strategy matters. You may think it's a no-brainer—of course, we need a strategy! But in my experience, a surprising number of organizations don't have annual budgets or capital plans or even set business rhythms, so why would they have a strategic planning process?

So, what's the case for strategic planning? There are two primary outcomes for the process. The first outcome is a plan. At the end of it, the organization should have a plan for what to do, where to spend its time, money, and energy, and how it will measure success. Those plans can help you guide the organization's choices over the next few years.

If done well, leaders will embed the strategy in the organization's other processes like budgeting, hiring, compensation, succession, and benefits. Your plan should articulate your company's secret sauce, identify how you will compete, how you will win, and what culture you will need to cultivate to do so. The plan should hold you accountable—we said this was important, did we do it? When looking across many research studies, analysts find that organizations that have formal strategic planning processes are more successful than those that don't. But common sense already tells us this—if you have a plan, you are more likely to achieve your goals than having no plan at all. It is the truth in our lives and in our organizations: hope is not a strategy.

The second outcome, which is probably more important than the first, is alignment. By going through a process of planning, you are bringing a group of senior leaders together to look at the same data, hear from a variety of voices and inputs, and make choices about the future of the organization. Going through a collaborative process helps create buy-in and makes it more likely people will make choices that support your shared goals. The more input you get from stakeholders, like board members, customers, or employees, the more it helps you address concerns and obstacles ahead of time. And by reviewing that plan on a regular basis, you help build agreement for other processes that may create conflict, such as who gets promoted, who gets a bonus, and how much gets spent on what capital projects. Strategic planning as a process helps reduce conflict because it creates higher alignment and clarity about what is important. Yes, the plan matters. But the process matters more.

Thus, the first step for any strategic planning process is to make the case for why strategic planning matters. In addition to why, you may get questions about how, who, and when. In the following pages, we will outline a simple process for the how—as for who and when, it depends on the organization. Strategic planning as a process is about finding the just-right place between speed and accuracy, influence and effectiveness. Too many people and you will go too slow. Not enough of the right people and you will not influence effectively or you may get the strategy wrong. Take too long and you may miss opportunities, go too fast and you may not get the buy-in you need. Different cultures may demand different levels of rigor, which add to the time and complexity of your process. Startup companies, like Dcode, operate in fast-moving environments that require flexible and fast planning processes composed of small teams, while fifty-year-old energy conglomerates may require months of careful development amongst numerous stakeholder groups and teams.

*2. Get the right people in the room.*

Remember, strategic planning is not just about producing a plan as quickly as possible—if no one cares, the process wastes time and money. Strategic planning is an influence process. As with any change, you must include the senior-most leaders, followed by their lieutenants, and then the key influencers in the organization. Ideally, these groups will all have a voice in the strategic planning process. If they don't have a voice, they may become obstacles or naysayers later, and then you will spend time having to convince them to support your plan. Why not just include them in some way from the beginning?

You may also have stakeholders you want to include in your strategic planning process. You could include key customers, vendors, partners, different employee groups, or high potentials who could develop greatly by being a part of the process. If you have a board, you should think through how to engage them. Some boards exist to provide governance and high-level strategic direction to the organization. Some boards are deeply enmeshed in the organization's operation. Some boards are there to open doors and raise money. Why your board exists should drive how deeply you involve them in the strategic planning process.

If you are in a family business, you may consider involving key family stakeholders or the next generation of family members. For all the reasons listed above, in a family business, which represent over 60 percent of the businesses, 60 percent of employees, and 60 percent of the US GDP, you should include people who may add to the conversation, or who may become immovable obstacles, or who could grow from the experience.

As Michael Porter, strategic planning guru, describes it, strategic planning is a process to do strategic thinking. When you consider whom to involve in the strategic planning process, ask which people you want to do strategic thinking together.

### 3. Get the right data.

Strategic planning is about looking at the past and the future, looking inside the organization and out. The process should give leaders a window into each of these, the opportunity to synthesize what they are learning and to develop a plan based on that data.

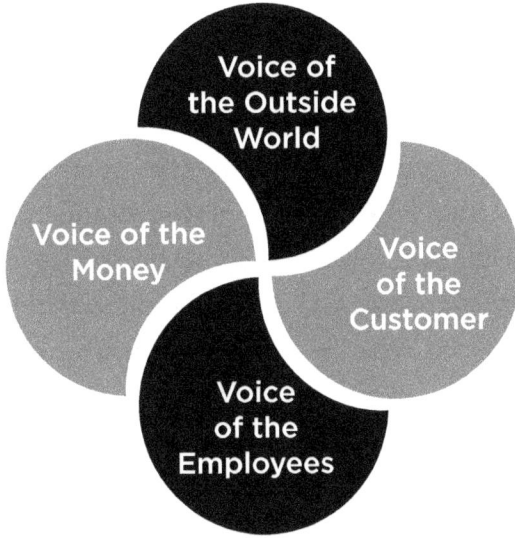

The first data you will need is financial—the voice of the money. Helpfully, it is often the easiest to obtain. How have we done financially over the past few years? What is our forecast for the next few years? Every organization prefers some metrics over others—some like net revenue, some like EBIDTA, and some like total dollars fundraised. Whatever financial data really matters to the business, get it and review it. The data you collect tells a story—your job is to read that story and make sense of it. The financials' voice should appear in the story the data is telling you—what is the voice of the money saying?

The second bit of data is the voice of the customer. Represent the voice of whoever buys and uses your services. Selling widgets to other businesses? Go ask those businesses what they think you are doing well and what you can improve. I always ask key leaders to talk to actual customers as part of the process, even if they are several steps removed from sales or are in support functions. They should have the voice of the customer in their head when making strategic planning decisions.

In addition to firsthand conversations, use whatever customer data you have that indicates how they feel about you. Have net promoter scores? Look at them. Have retention or customer churn data? Use it. Have demographics on who loves your products? Pay attention. Even as a service business or nonprofit, you can talk to clients. Serve another government agency or shared service group? Go talk to them. Raise money for needy children? Talk to their caregivers. Dcode wants to understand how three-star generals feel about their work. Ukrop's tracked customer feedback and used secret shoppers. Luck Companies collects customer feedback through surveys and conversations with the sales team, tracked within a customer relationship management system. YMCAs talk to donors, and school systems speak to parents.

When you talk to your customers or clients, try to find out what is going well and what is not. Strive to learn something new. Our own biases will prevent us from radically adjusting our opinions, so keep that in mind as your instincts tell you to dismiss what the customer tells you. Most people are nice and will not tell you to your face that your baby is ugly. But they will tell everybody else. Try to make it safe enough to glean useful feedback. If every customer tells you the organization is perfect, you are asking for feedback the wrong way. The customers' voice should appear in the story the data is telling you—what is that voice saying?

The third bit of data is the voice of the employees. You need to know how your employees feel. Do they feel great? Do they intend to stay? Are they looking for opportunities? Do they believe in you? Again, it is good to get firsthand experiences. Go talk to people. Listen to what they say. Again, your own biases will keep you from hearing contrary information, and it is easy to judge people for having a different experience than you think they should. When speaking to employees, lead with curiosity. They will likely share juicy nuggets of wisdom with you—if they are willing, have them describe your organization, warts and all, in their own words. If they feel afraid to share the unvarnished truth with you, that serves as an important data point for your strategy. Nothing extinguishes inspiration—the breath of life—like fear.

You can likely assume two things about your employee population. Number one, most of your employees want to be paid more money. That doesn't mean you have to pay them more, but no one walks around saying, "You know, I'm overpaid and want to make less." Even your $900,000 a year surgeon. Number two, your employees will say communication is a problem in your organization. (Because it always is. In every organization, every time.) This inconvenient fact may sound like hyperbole, but I have yet to encounter an organization where everyone feels like they are paid too much, and the communication is just too good.

Most organizations collect data that will help you understand what is going on inside the organization. How many people did we hire? How many people quit and why? How many did we fire and why? Promotions, performance review trends, turnover, and other employee data can all paint a picture of what's going on in the organization, as can employee engagement data or other surveys. The employees' voices should appear in the story the data is telling you—what is the voice of the employees saying?

The fourth bit of data is the voice of the outside world—basically, what is happening outside of your organization. What is happening in the economy? What are your vendors and suppliers experiencing? What are your regulators and tax bodies deciding? What's going on with your banks and investors? Again, a little firsthand knowledge goes a long way. Sit down with your key vendors and ask them what they see in the future. Ask your banker what is happening in their world. There is too much to learn out there, so get some firsthand knowledge and then learn what you can through reports, industry analysis, and other sources. The voice of the outside world should appear in the story the data is telling you—what is the voice of the outside world saying?

Around this time, you might be thinking, "I don't need any data because I have a good handle on what's happening inside and outside of my organization. I'm in touch—I have my finger on the pulse. I don't need to listen to any voices because the one in my head is telling me I'm right." It is healthy to pay attention to more voices than the one in your head. Yes, you may have a good grasp of what is going on inside and outside of your organization, but I doubt you have a complete grasp. We all have biases, blind spots, and preferences that filter out some data and focus on other data. We may be in danger of only seeing what we want to see, and hearing what we want to hear. The exercise of getting the right data is about adding to the data we already have, and systematically challenging what we think we know. The French believed the Maginot line was enough to stop the Germans even as the Germans were speeding past their fortifications; the British and the Germans greatly underestimated each other's radar systems, leading to untold casualties. Kodak invented the digital camera and got busy ignoring the seismic shift in their industry until it was way too late. We are all guilty of ignoring data—in fact, our brains are designed to do so. The only way of getting past this bias is by forcing ourselves to focus on it, even as we tell the voice in our head that while we are probably right, let's check to be sure.

### 4. Conduct a SWOT analysis.

As mentioned earlier in this book, a SWOT is a simple process for considering the organization's strengths, weaknesses, opportunities, and threats. It considers what is going on inside the organization as well as outside the organization. It should help you learn from the past and forecast the future. Your SWOT should help you synthesize what you have learned from the voice of the money, the voice of the customers, the voice of the employees, and the voice of the outside world. It should help you make sense of what you are seeing.

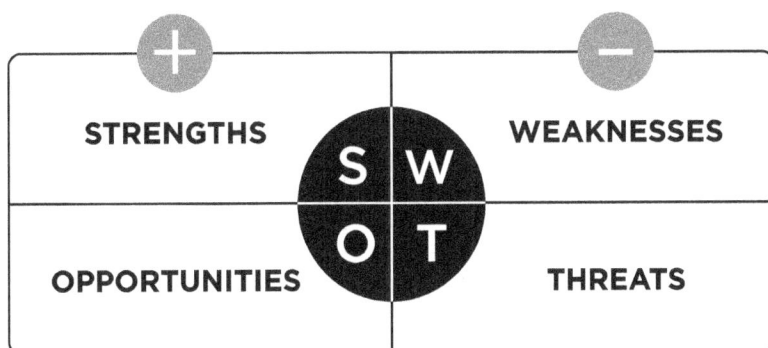

STRENGTHS — WEAKNESSES
OPPORTUNITIES — THREATS
S W O T

### 5. Challenge your assumptions.

SWOTs can be long and rigorous, or quick and dirty—but at a minimum, they should be a synthesis of the data we have collected about our organization and should help us challenge our assumptions of what we already know.

Human beings are designed to want to learn and simultaneously hate learning. We are excellent at ignoring data that challenges us, that undermines our current assumptions and beliefs. We have systemic biases built into our organizations in ways we are not aware of, based on our cultures. For example, if you have an engineering-based organization, everything will look like an engineering problem. I have seen engineering and architectural firms completely flummoxed by employees experiencing strong feelings and senior leaders either ignoring them or at a total loss of what to do. Luck Companies had decades of success based on operational efficiency, and it took multiple customers telling the company that quality alone was not enough to win their business in the future before the company took action.

We may be threatened by what the data is telling us and believe that it is wrong or rationalize it away. This has nothing to do with intelligence. Our brains love efficiency, skipping steps, and doing things in the easiest way possible. They are also resource hogs, and don't want to spend any extra energy learning from pesky facts that would require some serious rewiring. During the data collection phase, the SWOT, and even throughout the rest of the process, do not be surprised when people push back or worse, agree to everything positive and make no changes. Challenge yourself and your team to go beyond surface-level findings.

### 6. Bucket your conclusions.

Your strategic plan should help you leverage your strengths, address your weaknesses, take advantage of opportunities, and protect against threats. Your plan should also describe how you will utilize your organization's secret sauce (or customer value proposition). In the data, you will likely see trends and gaps, which will lead you to draw certain conclusions about what the future holds for your organization. Based on your data, you should come up with a handful of key areas that you want the organization to focus on over the next few years in response to your SWOT. These buckets form the major themes of your strategic plan. Some common buckets include growth, people, operations, and financials. Other areas might include innovation, sales, efficiency, or products. These themes ultimately become the core of your strategic objectives.

### 7. Determine your vision.

Again, your vision is that overarching goal that you want to accomplish during your next strategic planning window. Each of your strategic objectives—the buckets you chose earlier—serve the larger goal or vision you want to accomplish. Your strategic objectives and your vision should ultimately support the mission of the organization—why the organization exists. The plan components, just like the people, should align and hang together logically. Your vision should make sense to people NOT in the room. As Chris Yates says, "Can my ten-year-old explain it?"

Visions provide clarity to the organization—Where are we going? What are we trying to accomplish? Your strategy should answer the questions of "How are we going to get there? How are we going to accomplish our goal?" If visions inspire us, even better.

If they stretch us, great. If they are unclear, don't make sense, are impossible to achieve, or leave us feeling deflated, they don't work.

Mitchells, a family-owned company, includes high-end retail stores focused on men's and women's fashion. The vision of the organization is inspirational—to become one of the best specialty stores on the planet. At first glance, the vision seems unachievable—the best on the planet? Really? Yes, really. How do you measure it? Through available industry data. Is it possible? They are one of the few organizations that can make such a claim and achieve their vision. Will it stretch their associates? Of course.

The United States Drug Enforcement Agency, the DEA, intends to "enforce the controlled substances laws and regulations of the United States." They use the criminal and civil justice system of the US to stop the illicit flow of drugs into the country and support nonenforcement programs at home and abroad. As one DEA agent described it to me, "We fight bad guys all over the world who peddle drugs to kids, and we do it by kicking in doors and using calculators." While their official vision may not feel inspiring, the way they talk about it is. And more importantly, they mean it. Rarely have I experienced a more driven organization. And I love the idea that forensic accountants take down as many bad guys as the agents in the field do.

*8. Determine what success looks like.*

For your vision, how will you know you have been successful? How will you set the pace for how quickly you want to grow or how much you want to improve? How will you hold yourself and your organization accountable for achieving your strategy?

Goals and metrics, of course. Specifically, your strategic objectives and key performance indicators or KPIs. Remember the themes that you bucketed based on your SWOT? Use these themes to develop what you want to accomplish in your strategy, in support of your mission, values, and vision. Think of strategic objectives as the specific goals you set for the organization, and the KPIs as how you will measure your progress against your goals.

For example, imagine that you are a homebuilder focused on single-family homes in the mid-Atlantic. Your vision is to build one thousand homes a year. Your strategy for achieving this vision includes increasing operational efficiency in order to achieve a margin of 8 percent, developing three new home products that you will introduce into the coastal market to achieve $20 million in new revenue, retaining a talented workforce of sales, project managers, and designers, and lowering your voluntary turnover by 5 percent.

- Vision: build one thousand homes per year.
- Strategic Objectives: operational efficiency, new products, talent.
- Key Performance Metrics: 8 percent margin, $20 million in new revenue, lower voluntary turnover by 5 percent.

Establishing KPIs—or the measures of your goals—will help you Take Stock of the organization's progress in the future. Choosing your KPIs should be logical and straightforward. What data do we have easy access to that will provide us information about whether we are successful or not? What data will we use to adjust our organization over time? What information do we care about and will pay attention to in the future? Choose metrics that are too difficult to measure, and you won't use them. Choose metrics that you don't really care about, and you won't use them. Make things easy on your future self, because remember, you still have to lead this thing.

This is a good time to use forecasts to help set your overarching KPIs. What can you reasonably assume about the future, given all the data you have read and the story it has told you? Use these assumptions to set KPIs that stretch the organization; don't set metrics that employees find impossible to achieve, or goals so low that they don't require much effort. Know that no strategy is set in stone—strategic plans should be living and breathing documents you adjust over time based on what the data tells you as it changes.

Let's say your vision is to become the largest provider of home health care in the northeastern United States. Your strategic objectives include growth, client experience, financials, and operations.

The strategic objectives and KPIs might look something like:

- Growth: open three offices in Massachusetts by 2030.
- Client Experience: maintain a net promoter score of 90 percent year over year.
- Financials: grow top-line revenues by 10 percent year over year through organic growth within the Northeast.
- Operations: achieve gross margins across all offices in the Northeast of 15 percent by 2030.

*9. Develop tactics and a budget.*

Tactics include the steps you will take to achieve each of your strategic objectives. The tactics include projects that support your strategy and the actions beyond everyday operations that will allow you to achieve your goals. Tactics explain what we are going to do, who is going to do it, and when they are going to do it by. Tactics form a high-level project plan for your strategy. In the example above, the home health care company wants to achieve gross margins across all offices in the Northeast by 15 percent by 2030. What tactics will help you achieve this objective?

One tactic might be to conduct a review of all pricing for services and products across each of the major market areas in order to develop a competitive pricing plan for each market by 2027. Another tactic might be to establish a bonus program that rewards cost-saving ideas and promotes efficiency in 2028. A third tactic might be to implement and train office managers on a new scheduling system so that all offices can share home health care resources by 2027. The framework looks like this:

- Vision: become the largest provider of home health care in the northeastern United States.
- Operations Strategic Objective: achieve gross margins across all offices in the Northeast of 15 percent by 2030.
- Tactics:
  - Develop a competitive pricing plan for each market by 12/31/2027.
  - Establish a bonus program that rewards cost-saving ideas and promotes efficiency by 12/31/2028.
  - Implement and train office managers on a new scheduling system so that all offices can share home health care resources by 12/31/2029.

*9.5 Saying yes and saying no.*

Tactics include the actions you want to say yes to in support of your strategy—yet in most organizations the problem is not starting something, it is focusing on doing a few things well, which means saying no. Saying no is almost more important than saying yes—everything seems like a good idea in the planning phase, but when it comes to execution most organizations and people can only do a few things well. We overload our organizations with everyone's pet projects, politically expedient ideas, the misuse of extra resources, and projects we did not have the heart to kill off.

Our intentions tend to be mostly good—it is more fun to say yes than no. We claim to be data-driven then use the data to back up what we want to do anyway. Our results are okay enough to keep going and going and going but they tie up resources that could lead to breakthroughs in other areas. Sometimes we fear the repercussions of saying no because some stakeholder is in love with an idea, or we do not want to irritate customers, or we think a competitor will see an opportunity and pounce on us like a bear in the woods. As Charlie Luck, CEO of Luck Companies, warns us, "Be careful what you fall in love with." (He may also say, "Be careful who you fall in love with," but that is another book.)

Within the organization, we will have more ideas than the capacity to execute on those ideas. Any strategic planning process should include prioritizing the highest and best use of your time, money, and resources. One way to prioritize is to go through a subtraction process. As in Marie Kondo's book *The Life-Changing Magic of Tidying Up*, you want to throw out the things that don't bring you joy. No amount of organization will help you clean a cluttered house. Strategy is no different. No amount of organization will help you focus; only joyously and ruthlessly prioritizing the most important activities will make your organization successful. Which means subtracting tactics from your plan.

Two powerful, but underutilized strategic planning skills include focusing on a few things we can do exceptionally well and saying no. The strategic planning process, much like challenging our assumptions, should encourage us to be disciplined about what we say yes to initially. Over time, Taking Stock should keep us honest about what we can do, what is working and what is not, and inspire the leadership courage to end things that are not working out for the best. Remember Meagan Metzger's process at Dcode: keep, kill, double down, or modify.

Based on your vision, strategic objectives, key performance indicators, and tactics, you can assemble each of these pieces into an overall strategic plan. Your annual plan takes the portion of your strategy that you can see most clearly and boils down to what you can implement over the next twelve months.

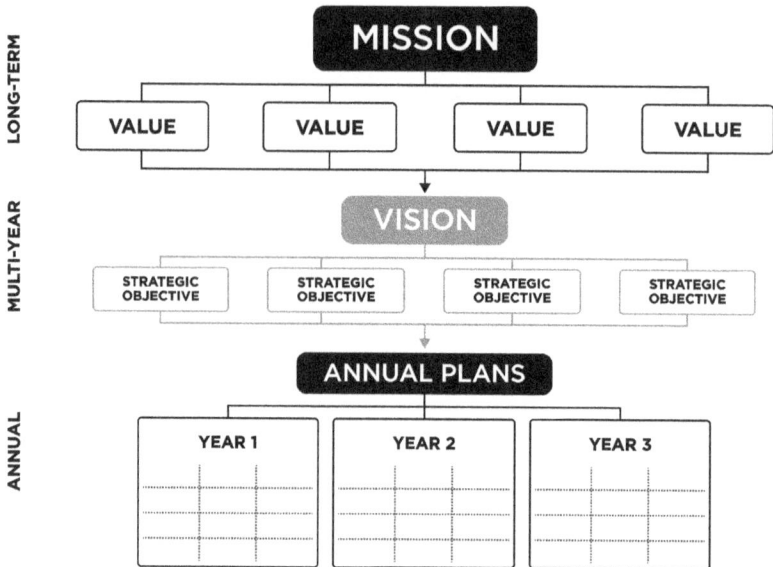

| LONG-TERM | | MISSION | | |
|---|---|---|---|---|
| | VALUE | VALUE | VALUE | VALUE |
| MULTI-YEAR | | VISION | | |
| | STRATEGIC OBJECTIVE | STRATEGIC OBJECTIVE | STRATEGIC OBJECTIVE | STRATEGIC OBJECTIVE |
| ANNUAL | | ANNUAL PLANS | | |
| | YEAR 1 | YEAR 2 | YEAR 3 | |

*10. Establish an organizational rhythm.*

Every organization has an internal calendar that determines when things happen. Outside forces like weather or tax season can influence our rhythms. State and federal agencies follow a legislative and budget process that influences when they have money to spend and when they do not. Industry trends make a difference as well—publicly held companies live and die by quarterly results; roads get paved in good weather, squeezing other activities into the winter; retail's busiest season in the United States happens between Thanksgiving and the New Year. Sometimes organizational rhythms are arbitrary because fifty years ago some CFO thought the fiscal year end should be June 1 so he could go to the beach and not worry. Schools in the United States still get summers off because when we built our education system a hundred years ago, most of the country's children needed to work on the farm during the growing and harvest seasons.

My advice is to be intentional about your organizational rhythms—what works best for you, your customers, and your industry. For example, in the construction business, housing starts predict the health of the industry. Most houses get built when the weather is nice—spring, summer, fall. Housing starts to fall off in the winter when the weather gets worse. Therefore, many construction companies try to jam in as much as they can into the winter months—training, communication, celebrations, large maintenance projects, and year-end parties—so they can focus on building things during the nice weather months. Weather drives the organizational rhythms of the construction world.

In general, leadership teams should review the results of their strategic plans once a quarter. Long enough to make progress, not so long that we get away from the plan. Then, once a year, revisit the strategy to make adjustments, typically when it makes sense. That adds up to three quarterly check-ins and one annual update. For example, since weather drives the construction industry, it would make sense to revisit a construction company's strategy in January, after all those year-end parties but before spring really starts to hit. That way the company can also set an annual budget and capital plan that supports the strategy early in the year. Then the company can check in on the progress of tactics and KPIs in the second, third, and fourth quarters.

Depending on your organization, the number of years you can look out highly depends on your industry. In the slower-moving construction industry, three- to five-year strategic plans are possible. In the fast-moving technology industry, one- to three-year strategic plans make more sense. Anything less than a year wouldn't provide the consistency or time that most businesses need to make progress. Any longer than five years turns into prophecy, not forecasting.

For strategic planning processes, some organizations can take six to eighteen months to develop a strategy. For others, a half-day offsite retreat is all they will invest. However, most organizations can spend a few days split up over a month or two to develop a mission, values, vision, and strategic plan if the process involves plenty of homework hearing the voice of the money, customers, employees, and the outside world.

Getting input and feedback provides a powerful way to pressure test your mission, values, vision, and strategic plan. Key stakeholders who have not been involved up to this point will feel like they can contribute without slowing the process down. By inviting input, you are also educating others on the mission, values, vision, and strategy before any official rollout. Consider it the soft launch of your strategy. A word of caution—don't ask for input if you don't want it and have no plans of incorporating it. You don't want to undermine the commitment you need from key people to accomplish your goals.

**KEY TAKEAWAYS**

To conduct successful strategic planning, we:

1.  Make the case for why.
2.  Get the right people in the room.
3.  Get the right data, including:
    A.  The Voice of the Money
    B.  The Voice of the Customer

      C. The Voice of the Employees

      D. The Voice of the Outside World

4. Conduct a SWOT analysis.

5. Challenge your assumptions.

6. Bucket your conclusions.

7. Determine your vision.

8. Determine what success looks like.

9. Develop tactics and a budget.

9.5. Say yes and say no.

10. Establish an organizational rhythm.

# CHAPTER FIVE

---

# Align Action, Part 2

Why else does Aligning Action matter?

If leaders and key stakeholders do not agree on a plan for the future, there is little chance an organization will successfully execute on its strategy.

Charlie Luck, CEO of Luck Companies, started his career in the early 1980s as a race car driver. "I had a cost structure of $250,000 to pay people, replace engines and tires, to travel, and everything. I had to find sponsors, to entertain their customers, introduce new products, and find ways to increase sales. There was no built-in demand, nobody cared if we went racing." When he joined Luck Companies, an aggregate producer and stone retailer based in the mid-Atlantic, he found a very different environment. "I had a P&L statement in 1979 for the racing team, and there was no shared P&L for our company beyond a few executives."

At the beginning of Charlie's tenure at Luck, the company did not share information like profitability with managers or salespeople. "It was just, 'Here are the categories, you manage the costs.'" At the time, the sales force focused on total revenue, which led to aggressive pricing but falling profitability since salespeople never saw the data. According to Charlie, "They were in the dark, running around with one leg tied up." And there was no incentive for sales to work with production, or vice versa. "We did a roll-up of a sales estimate and a price, then that was handed over to production to produce it."

As part of his entrance into Luck Companies, he attended a business program where a light bulb went off for him: he saw how the company could use data to make better decisions. By introducing ideas like business and strategic planning, the company could excel. "Stage one was understanding how to make money and how to run the business. Stage two was to run the business and have a multiyear strategy around what you wanted to do with particular people and growth."

The company did not have a defined culture at the time, but they did have themes for each year. "One year it was 'Do It Now.' Another year it was 'Save Fuel.' The following year it was 'The Customer Is the Boss.'" According to Charlie, those stickers ended up everywhere, on notepads and on the dashboards of haul trucks. The executives intended to send messages they felt mattered at the time but had no long-term defined cultural values.

As a result, Charlie brought in outside experts and charged one of his executives to learn everything he could about strategic planning and introduce it to the business. Charlie's role at the time was not to create the process, but to "prioritize it, yet throttle the evolution of the operating business so that people didn't choke." As the business evolved he saw plenty of people complaining, and "kicking the barn door" for having to do it. He also saw his higher performers get excited about optimizing the business. They were hungry for more information and wanted to make a bigger contribution to the company. A movement emerged as people sat around and talked about costs, revenues, and how to maximize profitability. A reinvention of the business had begun.

To recap, the Aligning Action process includes three steps:

- Evolving our vision and strategy
- Strengthening relationships
- Improving core processes

This chapter will focus on the second and third steps of Aligning Action: strengthening relationships and improving core processes.

## STRENGTHENING RELATIONSHIPS

Organizations are made up of people. People have different personality styles, different values, and different backgrounds, they look different, sound different, and come from different spaces, places, and economics. We are a world of difference. We have different strengths and aspirations, different weaknesses and failings. There are differences in pay, power, and decision-making.

Amidst all the differences, we also have different goals. Some of us want to win at all costs, others just want to be liked, some want to achieve, some want to help, some want to make oodles of money, and some want to make enough money to take care of their families. Motivations abound in any organization; businesses are not monoliths, and people are not mindless.

In some cases, employees like each other; in other cases, they don't. And just because leaders say, "We have a new strategy and we are moving in this direction" does not mean that anyone will take a single step forward. In some situations, leaders will resort to carrots and sticks, or rewards and discipline, to drive employee compliance. Like Alec Baldwin's character in *Glengarry, Glen Ross,* some leaders say to their sales teams, "First prize is a Cadillac El Dorado. Anyone wanna see second prize? Second prize is a set of steak knives. Third prize is you're fired."

In Values Based Organizations, we strive for more than just compliance; we want to earn the commitment of our teams. We want their commitment to make decisions that support our mission, values, vision, and strategy. Commitment does not come from rewards and discipline alone; it comes from our connection to others—from our relationships.

Every organization is in the people business. No matter where the money comes from, what the product is, or how the service is delivered, there are people behind the scenes making choices to buy it, sell it, agree to it, or use it. As a result, relationships are the most powerful force in organizations. For example, as DEA agents kick in doors and use calculators to fight bad guys around the world, they must build relationships with each other, with other agencies, with informants, with foreign governments we want to help stop the flow of drugs into the United States, and with police officers on the other side of the planet. They could not achieve their mission without relationships, and I would wager that the strength of their relationships determines the strength of their effectiveness as an agency.

From the research on organizations and leadership, we know that in teams and organizations:

- Where there is a lack of trust, we see much lower performance.
- Where there is a sense of psychological safety, there is much higher performance.
- Where there is poor communication between individuals, opportunities and mistakes get missed.
- Where employees feel a sense of belonging, they are more engaged and as a result use more of their discretionary effort to help others.
- Where relationships are dysfunctional and toxic, complete with infighting and sabotage, we see much worse results.
- Where relationships are healthy, we see much better results.

None of this research says we should all hold hands and sing songs and pet puppies and kittens (unless that's your business model). However, the research does provide a strong case for the return on investment of relationship building; it is worth leaders' time and effort to strengthen their relationships and encourage others to do the same. We buy from people we like. We help the people who will help us. We want to be accepted by others. We want to be part of the group. We can build organizations where ideas are challenged, high performance is expected, and low performance is not tolerated, where people are committed to the work and all have strong relationships. The military has long understood the value of unit cohesion and morale. Sports teams understand winning requires chemistry between the players. In physics, force multipliers are tools that reduce the amount of force to move an object. In organizations, relationships are force multipliers when they are good, and force inhibitors when they are bad. If our goal is to move people in a specific direction, relationships reduce the amount of work it takes to align their actions.

To strengthen relationships, do an audit of those you have strong relationships with, and those with whom you do not. A leadership theory we have studied since the 1960s, Leader Member Exchange theory, argues that leaders have high-quality exchanges with some people and low-quality exchanges with others. The quality of the relationship benefits leaders, as high-quality exchanges lead to the results they want, while low-quality exchanges lead to worse results. The quality of the relationship benefits followers as well, as high-quality exchanges lead to better assignments and rewards, while low-quality exchanges lead to fewer opportunities and even exclusion from the group.

Consider which relationships you need to build and those you need to strengthen. In the sales world, it is common to have a plan for who will build a relationship with particular influencers within a company. At Dcode, Meagan Metzger may have a plan to build a relationship with a new three-star general in the Space Force. At Kenmore, Scott pitches his company to firms in New York while Kristin focuses on her plant's team leads. As a part of a relationship audit, and ultimately Aligning Action, consider the network and ask questions. Who will connect with the estimators and purchasing agents? Who will connect with the field supervisors or department heads? Who will connect with the CEO? Yet in leadership, we don't often think this way. We either hope that we will have the relationship equity we need when we need it, or we vastly underestimate how much relationships impact our ability to influence others to take action. Hope, as we have said, is not a strategy.

Relationships that build commitment are more than transactional; to build commitment you need to build trust. Relationships require empathy—understanding why someone feels the way they do—and getting to know others beyond surface-level observations. Building commitment requires more than just meeting your own needs—focusing on the success of other people will open a door to relationships with them. To do so, we must adapt our approach to the person and the situation. For some people, the challenge feels easy because you already have similar values and you get along like best friends. For others, it will be more work. However, the effort is worth it. Beyond the fact that healthy relationships yield awesome results for our sense of satisfaction and health, awesome relationships have a clear business benefit. If we want to align actions and improve our ability to influence, it will require strengthening relationships.

Early in the values journey at Luck Companies, leaders realized they must care about others in order to lead. This came as a surprise to many; they asked, "Do we need to care about the people we like, or do we have to care about everybody?" They also asked, "How can we care about others in a male-dominated blue-collar business?" As it turns out, you can care about people in any industry, in ways that feel meaningful to them—care about who they are, what they dream about, and what they need to be successful.

Actively caring about others even as you hold them accountable, even as you give them the toughest feedback they have ever had in their lives, is part of the magic of leading well. As Guy Clumpner has found in his work with Holt Caterpillar, the San Antonio Spurs, and with clients throughout the US: if you make people feel like they matter, they will do great things.

## IMPROVING CORE PROCESSES

There are lots of reasons why organizations don't work as well as they should. Often the various pieces, parts, people, and departments do not align. They work suboptimally at best or against each other at worst. Systems, and the processes that support them, are no different.

Let's say your goal is to provide outstanding customer service over the phone to your customers. But you reward your employees for the number of calls they complete in a day, which results in getting customers off the phone as quickly as possible. Your process of rewards does not align with your goal of service.

Another goal may be for your production team to work collaboratively with your sales team. But your production team only communicates up to the Director of Operations, and the sales team only communicates up to the Director of Sales. Your process of communications does not align with your goal of collaboration.

Yet another goal could be to raise money from your largest donors. But you don't have an effective way of tracking who donated and why. Your process of donor relationship management does not align with your goal of raising money.

To successfully achieve a vision and strategy, or to live into a mission and transform a culture, you need processes that will deliver the results that you want. If you want a collaborative culture, how do your work processes encourage teamwork? If your vision is to be the safest hospital for patients, how do your cleaning protocols create a safe environment? Mission, values, vision, and strategy are all outcomes that you want to deliver—and often we have not scrutinized our processes with these ends in mind.

Once an organization grows beyond the early founders, reaching a certain size, the organization ceases to function well until it establishes processes to drive consistency. As a startup with two people, you can get away with not having a compensation strategy. As a fifty-year-old manufacturing business with one thousand employees, you can't, at least not well. Processes in many organizations emerge organically—someone had a problem, solved it, and the solution sticks around for years. Why we do what we do gets lost over time as people quit, retire, or move on to different roles. For example, engineers designed the space shuttle's rocket boosters to fit on railroad tracks designed by engineers to fit on Roman roads that you could fit two donkeys on side by side. On the Windows operating system, designers shaped the save button like a floppy disk, which people under the age of twenty-five have never used or even seen before. (Don't get me started on the clipboard as a copy-and-paste icon.) We focus so much on putting out the day's fires that we don't take the time to overhaul our processes to align with our goals.

Most organizations have hundreds of processes, compounding the problem. Organizational structure is a type of process in this case. Who reports to whom, what roles people play, and how decisions get made are processes that may or may not support what we want.

What to do? Prioritize improving the core processes that most directly support your mission, values, vision, and strategy. Some key areas where many organizations fall short include:

1. How are people rewarded? If you are not rewarding people for acting in ways that support your goals, improve these processes.
2. How do people communicate? If the right information is not being received by the right people at the right time, improve these processes.
3. How do decisions get made? If decisions are not being made at the lowest level possible in an organization, everything slows down or people wind up disempowered. If decisions are ill-informed or have ineffective results, improve these processes.
4. What is our structure? If there is not clarity in who reports to whom and the structure doesn't make sense, improve these processes.
5. What is our customer experience? If you are not easy to do business with, improve these processes.
6. What is our employee experience? If your turnover is too high or you struggle to recruit talent, improve these processes.

One of the outcomes leaders clamor for is accountability. We complain endlessly that the right people are not held accountable for the right things. Accountability in organizations has three components:

- Clear goals and expectations
- Feedback on performance against those goals and expectations
- Rewards and consequences that align with performance against goals and expectations

If you don't have all three in your organization, you don't have accountability. What makes it tricky is that accountability is a leadership outcome, a cultural outcome, and a process outcome. There are leadership issues when people aren't held accountable (lack of goals, lack of feedback, lack of rewards and consequences), cultural issues (everyone is too nice or doesn't trust management), and process issues (no ways to reward high performers or exit low performers). Accountability as leadership, as culture, and as process should be tackled as part of any major organizational change, and especially in a Values Based Organization. And ultimately, you can't Align Action without processes like accountability.

For more about accountability, keep reading.

**KEY TAKEAWAYS**

To Align Action, we:

- Evolve our vision and strategy
- Strengthen relationships
- Improve core processes

# CHAPTER SIX

# Champion Values Based Leadership

Why Champion Values Based Leadership?

You cannot align an organization without leadership, and without alignment, organizations prove less effective no matter the measure.

■ ▯ ▮

"I have a simple metric that I use with people all the time," says Guy Clumpner, President of Holt Development Services, Inc. "When you have four people in a family unit, you have the possibility of eleven subrelationships. And that's why people in a four-person family can't agree on pizza for dinner. And when that group gets to twenty-four people, you have the potential for 17.6 million subrelationships. I look at the sheer number of employees and locations we have, and I see a ton of organizational complexity."

For thirty-five years, Holt Caterpillar, the largest Caterpillar dealership in the United States and a multibillion-dollar organization, has been on a Values Based Leadership journey. The company has dedicated decades of time and resources to hone its culture and equip its leaders with the tools necessary to lead in a Values Based Organization. The company uses the values to provide clarity and reduce the variability of relationships across the organization, and leadership tools to increase alignment despite a large number of locations and geographic spread.

Holt offers standard leadership workshops as well as a two-year leadership development program. Leaders must display mastery of four domains: self-management, adaptability, learning agility, and technical acumen. "If you don't have a pretty clear mastery of those, you just won't have a prayer to get promoted in the organization," says Guy.

One of the skills Holt teaches leaders and promotes is the willingness to have tough and clear conversations—starting with questions, of course. "When you get into the habit of asking questions, everything becomes a conversation. I can go into a criticizing mindset, which is self-defeating, or I can say, 'I care about you and I want to help you be successful.'" Then leaders ask questions to understand their strengths and gaps. They try to honor the choices employees make to close those gaps or not. According to Guy, employees have 100 percent control over their destiny—if they don't have the commitment to close their gaps, then Holt honors their choice to work somewhere else.

Although they have been on the path for years, "it's a never-ending journey." They keep the values work alive through big things like their ongoing development programs and little things like practices and rituals. "Every meeting starts with a safety briefing followed by values in action stories," says Guy. "Every meeting, large, small, with customers, without customers, at the headquarters, stores, and branch locations." This habit helps reinforce what the organization supports, endorses, and enforces. They also have an orientation toward collaboration and catching people doing things right. According to Guy, it allows Holt to "hire and retain really, really talented people who take an ownership mindset to the culture.

"It's basic reciprocity," says Guy. "When I feel like I matter, then I pay that forward to our external customers, to the community, to our investors, to all stakeholder groups."

One of the essential ingredients of any Values Based Organization is leadership. Just as values guide organizations, values guide our choices. Except in this case, Values Based Leaders live, work, and lead in alignment with their personal core values and the values of the organization. They do so to ignite the potential of others and to lead the organization to its highest levels of performance, effectiveness, and impact.

When it comes to VBL, leadership is a choice, not a title. We have all known leaders with big titles and corner offices who could not lead their way down the hall, much less build the kind of commitment that inspires people to walk through walls for them. The impact of leaders across any organization cannot be understated—research shows us time and again that leadership matters. It matters to productivity, performance, trust, culture, safety, innovation, customer service, teamwork, and on and on. On almost every measure, effective leadership has a positive impact on organizational outcomes.

In any organization, leaders can help the organization thrive or fail based on how they lead their teams. In Values Based Organizations, leaders have a responsibility to do everything in their power to help their employees succeed. They understand how their choices impact others in the short- and long-term. As leadership has an impact on the alignment of culture and strategy, organizations should focus on it as part of any process. Thus, in order to Champion Values Based Leadership, we:

- Develop leadership strength
- Influence key people
- Hold self and others accountable

### DEVELOP LEADERSHIP STRENGTH

Show me an organization that underperforms, and I will show a leader who underperforms. Moreover, I will show you an organization vastly underusing its talent. Since leadership is a choice, not a title, everyone can choose to lead. At every level. Everyone can make a positive impact on the lives of others at work. But can the formal leaders harness this power and turn this untapped potential into positive outcomes?

Values Based Organizations require leaders to execute on strategic plans, establish visions, transform cultures, and lean into the mission of the organization. Leadership is absolutely critical to taking values from a pretty poster on the wall to something an organization uses to make decisions and guide processes. Leadership is also required to make the hard calls that will move the organization toward higher performance and accountability.

Leadership, however, is not something that most organizations have an overabundance of. Why? Because most organizations have not invested the time and energy into developing the leadership strength they need to transform their organizations. They have not attracted the kind of talent that allows them to manage increasingly complex situations. They have not built the bench strength needed to lead in the future.

Jim Kouzes, co-author of *The Leadership Challenge*, compares developing leaders to developing baseball players. "When do we typically start developing baseball players and future Hall of Famers?" he asks. "Four or five years old. And when do we start developing leaders?" Typically, when they are in their twenties, and managing people for the first time. If leadership is so crucial to our organizations, why wait so long to develop these critical skills? It is no wonder organizations struggle to invest the time, money, and effort required to develop the leadership skills of their employees. They are paying for a lifetime of missed opportunities.

In our book, *InnerWill: Developing Better People, Braver Leaders, and a Wiser World through the Practice of Values Based Leadership* (Epperson, 2022), we describe how to develop Values Based Leaders using Five Practices:

1. Building Awareness
2. Realizing Potential

3. Developing Relationships
4. Taking Action
5. Practicing Reflection

**Building Awareness** requires looking in the mirror and seeing ourselves clearly, including our strengths and weaknesses. When we build awareness, we explore our values, our personality style, our beliefs and assumptions, and how all of these shape our behaviors and the choices we make.

**Realizing Potential** means developing our purpose, the overarching "why" of our lives. To reach our potential and live into our purpose, we must strive toward becoming the best version of ourselves.

**Developing Relationships** calls for building trust with others. By understanding their values, style, and needs, and adapting our approach, we can become more effective influencers and communicators.

**Taking Action** means making conscious choices that align with our values and the values of the organization. We run toward the fire, not away from it, choosing to have the hard conversations and to do the difficult work of leaders.

**Practicing Reflection** includes pausing to consider our impact on others. Did we adapt our approach? Did we act on our values? Were we effective? After reflecting, we should apply the lessons learned through successes and failures.

Values Based Leadership requires that we personally build

the capacity to lead over time. It means working on our self-awareness, our relationships, and our ability to adapt to people and situations—to make conscious choices and to learn from the past. It does not mean we are bad; you don't have to be bad to be better. It does mean making a few more conscious choices each day, choices that align with our values and the impact we want to make. By championing Values Based Leadership, we get a little bit better throughout our lives—making leadership choices happens at work, at home, and in our communities.

Early in my career, I valued competence above all. If I judged that you weren't competent, I was not interested in what you had to say or what you thought, and I certainly did not care how you felt. In my thinking, feelings had nothing to do with business. I believed "It's not personal, it's business" was the right way to run any organization. I thought relationships were overrated, probably because I was bad at them. I thought that the world was a meritocracy where the best efforts, the hardest workers, and the best ideas won out.

I was wrong.

Yes, I was a hard worker. I was committed. I was smart. I had many strengths. But I was no leader. I did not understand my style or my values. My emotional intelligence was nearly nonexistent—I would joke that I had one feeling and you couldn't hurt it. I certainly couldn't pick up on the emotional cues of others. (Your eyes are sweating. That's weird.) I could not see my weaknesses, or how my direct, overly task-focused style negatively impacted others.

Ultimately, I did not know how to lead with a vision, to inspire commitment, or how to influence others. I was fortunate enough to be a part of an organization—Luck Companies—that went through a cultural and leadership transformation just at the time that I needed it personally and professionally. The organization has invested deeply in me becoming a better person, and braver leader, and has encouraged me to support a wiser world. Because of this investment, I have grown so much more effective than at the beginning of my career. More adaptable, better able to build relationships, more effective in influencing others, able to give and get feedback, able to set expectations and hold others accountable. It required an investment in my horizontal skills—technical skills like budgeting—and my vertical skills, the skills required to be a high-functioning human being. The organization continues to invest in me and raises the bar on my leadership year after year after year.

In most of our careers, we go through a period of rapid development, especially in new jobs or companies. Events in our lives can spur growth: marriages, births, deaths, parenthood, aging parents, divorces, and breakups. Life gives us lessons if we practice reflection. Others also can help us learn—mentors, therapists, doctors, and friends. We can learn spiritually and emotionally in our places of worship and in our community. We also unintentionally pick up a few more skills along the way just by living.

It is possible to go through these events and not develop as people. Outside of new jobs, our development slows to a trickle. Unless we are the type of person who always learns, we tend to stagnate. Our leadership skills grow stale, and we lean on what might have worked a few decades earlier. If we want to build a Values Based Organization, however, and we don't want to wait a lifetime to do it, we can intentionally develop our leadership strength.

Let's start with why developing leadership strength in your organization matters. Values Based Organizations require leadership to transform their cultures, to set the example for others to follow, to execute strategies, and to lean into their missions. Without enough leadership horsepower aligned on accomplishing the same goals, these efforts fail. As a formal leader, it is important to articulate why your organization should invest in developing leaders, both to secure the time, energy, and funding to do so and to show participants why it is worth their efforts.

Now let's define what leadership skills to develop. The organization's mission, values, vision, and strategy give us a blueprint for what unique skills our leaders need. All leaders need basic skills such as goal setting, giving and getting feedback, communication skills, and developing others. Some leaders will need more advanced skills such as setting a vision, dealing with conflict, influencing others, leading teams, and strategic thinking. A few leaders will also need high-level skills such as navigating polarities or guiding complex systems.

Your values and the culture you want to create will require additional leadership skills. For example, if one of your values is creativity then leaders will need skills such as innovation, design thinking, and leading through change. If one of your values is efficiency then your leaders may need skills grounded in SixSigma, root cause analysis, or one-to-one production.

Your strategy may also drive different leadership behaviors. For example, if your business strategy is high-touch customer service, your leaders will need to know how to thrill customers. If you have a sales strategy, your leaders will need to develop high-performing sales teams or build connections with key customers.

One of the biggest challenges of new strategies stems from the organization's core competencies. Often, companies pursue strategies related to their existing core competencies. Apple used its competencies of design and technology to put a computer chip into a phone and revolutionized that industry, while BlackBerry resisted adding such power-hungry and expensive technology. Consumers, they insisted, loved their keyboards even as their share of the phone market dropped to nearly zero.

However, sometimes companies pursue strategies outside of their core competencies with mixed results. In these cases, "the downside of execution is that you are going to have to build a new set of competencies," says Bob Kelley, former COO of Ukrop's Super Markets. Transformative strategies demand new skills that the organization must either recruit for or develop, along with new mindsets for senior leaders and beyond.

- When GM started its Saturn line of cars in response to the proliferation of affordable Japanese sedans in the United States, it launched it as a "different kind of car company." They chose new platforms to build the car on, new materials within the cars, and an entirely new way of selling cars: no-haggle pricing. GM had to develop entirely new core competencies to design, build, and sell these cars. Wildly successful at first, senior leaders within GM never really embraced the "different kind of car company" mindset, and cannibalized what made Saturn great, replacing it with the old GM way of doing things. Over time, and with the economic catastrophe of 2008, GM ultimately closed its Saturn operations for good in 2009.

- Luck Companies realized that to compete in the future, leaders would need to grow comfortable using technology and data to drive business decisions. Throughout its history, the company collected reams of data, but leaders relied on their intuition to make key decisions. To build this new core competency, the company invested in digital dashboards, recruited a team of data scientists, set new expectations for associates, and promoted leaders who showed the ability to incorporate technology into their daily work. While imperfect, the company has made great strides in building data competency.

- For the past several years, Microsoft has pursued cross-platform technology. In the past, product lines stayed siloed—a programmer working on Word did not need to cross-pollinate with Outlook. However, in the future, the company's offerings will grow more and more integrated, which means leaders will need the skills to break down silos, communicate across teams, and lead their employees in a highly networked environment.

Once we have identified the skills leaders need to develop, we need a process for how we develop leadership strength in the organization. Organizations employ a wide variety of methods of developing leaders. For example, you could follow the 70/20/10 rule where 70 percent of development happens on the job, 20 percent in the classroom, and 10 percent through coaching and mentoring. You can give leaders special assignments and projects that focus on a few key behaviors and skills. You can get them a coach or a mentor, where they would work on their goals one-on-one. You could send them to online classes, retreats, and workshops. Different approaches work better for different individuals.

While there are many approaches to leadership development, at InnerWill we prefer taking a cohort of leaders through a shared experience, where they get the benefits of working in a group along with the benefits of working on their own. We have found that the group has insights that they share with one another, that their relationships can help them sustain change outside of the classroom, and that they build public commitment and accountability to the people they work with. When paired with individual or small group coaching, participants learn powerful insights about themselves and others. We also prefer leaders to work on real-world challenges—such as developing a new business strategy, turning around a failing project, or understanding key customer needs while working on their leadership skills. We don't believe in fake scenarios or role-playing—the more we can ground it in practical reality, the better.

Developmental experiences should raise the stakes by feeling real and useful. Adult learners will quickly bail out of an exercise if it smells inauthentic or too trivial. Building in time to practice reflection throughout the development process helps learners identify what leadership lessons they are learning and how to build on them in the future. We also like including opportunities to practice their skills—such as giving and getting live feedback, alongside assessment instruments like 360 Degree surveys based on competencies that support the organization's culture and strategy.

## INFLUENCING KEY PEOPLE

Influence results in action. As formal leaders, our job includes influencing the choices other people make in support of what the organization wants to accomplish. For example, if we want someone to show up to work on time, we influence them to do so, typically with rewards or punishments. Centuries ago, farmers would try to influence their donkeys to move by hanging carrots in front of them, and if they still did not move, they would encourage them with sticks. As leaders, we have many more tools than carrots and sticks to influence others.

Most of the experts interviewed for this book, including Bob Kelley, John Pullen, Chris Yates, and Guy Clumpner, believe mindset serves as a roadblock or an accelerator to transformational change, culture work, and strategic planning. "Before I do anything whether it's brand, culture, or strategy, I work on unfreezing the leadership teams, creating readiness," says Bob Kelley. "Most of us operate in paradigms: we wake up, go to work, come home, go to bed. We get in this flow. Most people like their paradigm, but it's a concrete box that resists change. How can we chip away at that box to open them up to new possibilities?"

As Bob looks at companies that are currently struggling, he sees a fixed mindset, a concrete box that leaders will need to chip away at before they can change. "Look at Red Lobster, Peloton, Beyond Meat. They are struggling to figure out their next pivot and create a business model that works." In any kind of major change, according to Bob, "you're going after what made their brands great. How do you get someone ready to hear that they are no longer relevant?"

Influence, in this case, creates readiness for change by encouraging a new mindset. When Luck Stone moved away from an operations-focused business to a customer-focused business, John Pullen had to tackle the organization's mindset through influence. He shared data, including the voice of the customer and the voice of the external world, he told stories, and he painted a vision of what the organization could be and how everyone fit within it. "We had to spend a lot of time on belief creation about why we're doing it and that it wasn't just flavor of the month." With his clients, Bob Kelley leads strategic thinking workshops, has teams read articles, and encourages participants to experience other businesses and cultures, like taking CEOs surfing after visiting REI's headquarters for a discussion about sustainability. Like John Pullen and Bob Kelley, there are a variety of influence tools at your disposal to aid in influencing mindsets and ultimately action.

## MODELING

Modeling serves as the most important tool in our influence toolbox. Senior leaders must model what they want and set an example for others to follow. In my experience, professional boss watchers fill our organizations. Leaders always stand on stage, while employees constantly check if the audio—what they say—and the video—what they do—align. Whether you call it walking the talk or checking if the audio matches the video, the result of a leader who says one thing and does another undermines any cultural change. Too much distance between a leader's words and actions causes employees to grow cynical or feel that the system is rigged and unfair. Expecting others to support organizational values or a new strategy when employees do not trust the leader to support them leads to resistance—sometimes passive aggressively and sometimes aggressive aggressively. As one of our most powerful tools, we should strive to model what we expect.

Stories abound of senior leaders preaching frugality and cutting jobs while spending lavishly on perks—of CEOs who choose a successor then work to undermine them. Of leaders saying integrity matters then lying, cheating, or stealing. The impact of these choices grows beyond cynicism; it undermines employee engagement, which lowers employee commitment, which leads to turnover at best and felonies at worst. Leaders will not be perfect; "We are human beings, not perfect beings," as Guy Clumpner likes to say. Yet Values Based Leaders must hold themselves to the highest standards in the organization—admitting when they fail and taking responsibility for their actions in all cases.

While powerful, modeling is not the only influence tool we have in our leadership toolkit. As described in the Steps of Learning in an earlier chapter, influence starts with awareness. Our job is to help employees understand that a change is coming. You can do this through big organization-wide parties, a series of videos, blogs on the topic, or small group meetings where you describe the change. The point is to help employees see that a change is coming and that it will impact them. Once they are aware, we move on to understanding, which may include training, workshops, or simple storytelling. As we influence, we are building to acceptance—when employees believe that a change is for the best and are willing to act in support of the change. We can position change as positive or negative, as incremental or huge, but influence begins with communicating. So what are our communication influence tools?

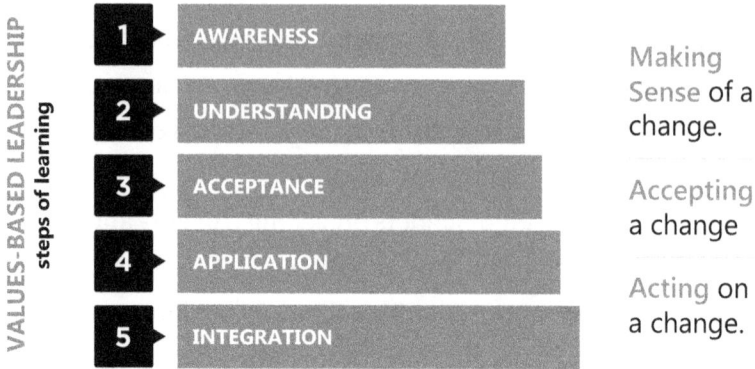

| VALUES-BASED LEADERSHIP<br>steps of learning | | | |
|---|---|---|---|
| 1 | AWARENESS | Making Sense of a change. |
| 2 | UNDERSTANDING | |
| 3 | ACCEPTANCE | Accepting a change |
| 4 | APPLICATION | |
| 5 | INTEGRATION | Acting on a change. |

|¦| INNERWILL

## TELLING PEOPLE

You would be amazed how often leaders neglect to tell their people about upcoming changes. We get in a hurry, we get busy, we forget. We assume others will read our minds or will "pick up what we are putting down," even though we aren't putting anything down. Or we assume telling our people once is enough. As a child, how many times did your parents tell you to clean your room, eat your vegetables, or stop swearing, and how often did you do exactly as you were told? As adults, plenty of experts tell us we should eat right, exercise, get plenty of sleep, and avoid sugar, salt, fat, and fun in our lives, but how many of us consistently do all these things because someone told us?

In marketing, experts often tout the Rule of 7. The Rule of 7 argues that consumers need to hear about a product seven times before buying it. Communication experts have taken this to mean we should expose our audience to an idea seven times before they will act on it. Originating as an advertising maxim in the 1930s, this idea has persisted for nearly one hundred years for a reason. The reason? One and done is never enough. Telling someone once is not influencing; telling them again and again encourages action. In my own team, I spent over a year repeating the mantra "Customers come first." Should we start a new program? Customers come first. Spend money on a new software package? Customers come first. Fly out at 5:00 a.m.? Customers come first. It got so bad that during the holidays my team bought me a mug with the caption "Tom Comes Last." Apparently, a good rule of thumb about how often you need to tell someone: enough times that your audience starts to make fun of you about it. Then say it a few more times just to be sure.

### SHARING HOW WE FEEL

Emotions are powerful influence tools. If you can connect someone emotionally to an idea, they will be much more likely to act on it. One of my team led the development of the commercial for the ASPCA where Sarah McLachlan sings "In the Arms of an Angel" while showing pictures of animals who have been mistreated. The ASPCA raised a great deal of money from that campaign because people love dogs, and they responded emotionally to the commercial. If you want someone to make a different choice, it must be more than logical, it must be emotional. In their fantastic book *Switch*, Chip and Dan Heath describe influence as a man riding an elephant. You must convince the rider by appealing to logic and facts, you have to encourage the elephant through emotions, and you have to shape the path the elephant and rider travel on. Sharing how you feel, especially through our own vulnerability, connects us to others and makes it more likely others will act. Influence requires more than just logic.

"We have to fall in love," says Chris Yates. "People need to feel an emotional understanding of why we are doing a strategy." During his tenure at a global heavy equipment manufacturer, the company wanted to make progress possible in the world. "We would show videos of a remote village in India," said Chris, "where women had to get water from a well outside of the village, which was dangerous because they could be hurt, raped, kidnapped, or killed. One day one of our generators shows up, and the village has electricity for the first time in their lives. Someone strings lights from the village to the well. You see the children, the people, and you go, "That's why we come to work every day."

At a global technology company, Chris shared that "we were about empowering the world. We would tell the story of a boy who couldn't play video games with his friends at Christmas because he was born without thumbs and fingers. We developed a different kind of controller that responds without hands. Suddenly this boy is empowered to have a life socially with his friends. You tell this story again and again and bring your purpose to life."

## TALKING ABOUT WHY

"Because I said so" isn't anywhere near good enough for parents, bosses, or presidents as an influence tool. Adults want to understand why they should make a different choice. They want to know the rationale and the stakes behind the choices they will make. The why can include a simple statement of the benefits of such a choice. It could also be an inspirational appeal to something greater than us.

The parable of the stone cutters—based on Christopher Wren rebuilding St. Paul's cathedral in London after the Great Fire of the 1600s—describes an architect asking three masons what they are doing. One answers that he is working to feed his family, the other answers that he is building a wall, and the third says he is building a cathedral to the Almighty. Leadership gurus like to say this parable should encourage employees to find the cause greater than themselves as they make doorknobs or audit tax returns. I would encourage you to be ruthlessly pragmatic as you talk about why. Find what works for your audience and say that. Feeding your family can be motivation enough and without walls, there would be no cathedrals.

## TELLING STORIES

Stories can paint a picture of the future, what things could look like, or explain the impact of an action without dryly reciting facts. Stories are sticky; we recall them more easily than facts. Telling a story that vividly describes a change inspires action when facts fail. In our business, no amount of facts can convince someone to believe in leadership. However, stories about the personal impact of leadership can sway the hardest hearts. Howard Schultz, former CEO of Starbucks, would frame the company's values using stories about growing up poor in Brooklyn. Steve Jobs launched the iPod by telling stories about carrying one thousand songs in your pocket. Sheryl Sandberg wrote an international bestseller describing her own story with the intent of championing women leaders. Stories move us.

Mark Twain is alleged to have said, "Never let the truth get in the way of a good story." He also is alleged to have said, "Nothing spoils a good story like the arrival of an eyewitness." Politicians love to tell stories about real people who don't exist, and if they do exist, did not do the thing they said. Leaders tell made-up stories at their own risk. These stories undermine our influencing efforts—especially if they increase cynicism and distrust. Leaders ground the best stories in reality—and tell them in a way that makes us see what they see, feel what they feel, and act as they act.

## ASKING QUESTIONS

If the change is large enough, people will have opinions. If they aren't sharing them with you, they are sharing them with someone else. Influence includes leaving people feeling heard, which means asking questions and leading with curiosity. Of course, asking questions assumes that you listen to the answers. Leaving others feeling heard often builds enough trust that the audience will try something new. Not hearing others typically leads to resentment and resistance, two very difficult states to change.

Questions build engagement, which leads to input and ideas. When you incorporate others' ideas into a strategy or change of any kind, it tends to build buy-in from the people you ask. Also, questions can help you understand how others feel, giving you more data to take action or to increase the effectiveness of your influence. Being curious invites others in. As Guy Clumpner says, "You can take a more Socratic approach and ask questions. People will literally tell you everything, predicated on your ability to learn and listen. You can learn about their intentions. You can learn about their fears, about their concerns, about their mindset."

Most of us want to have a say in how our workplaces operate. Many leaders argue that they know best, that they have more information than their people, and that they should be the final arbiters of any strategy. These assumptions can lead to poor choices and the wrong plan. And people hate feeling as if something is being done *to* them, as opposed to *with* them. If we feel like the victim of a change, with no ability to influence the outcome, we will resist it.

Consider the major changes many of us go through: serious relationships, marriages, having children, switching jobs, and moving to new states and new countries. Often, we make these changes with a sense of excitement and joy. Yet when we feel others control us, we resist passively by moving slowly or not putting in the extra effort large-scale change requires. We resist actively by complaining, quitting, or undermining new processes. We don't move forward with enthusiasm and may act in compliance but with little commitment. As leaders, we strive for commitment not just compliance. By asking questions, we gain the information we need to earn the commitment of others to act.

You can influence new mindsets by using the tools above, including:

- Modeling
- Telling people
- Sharing how we feel
- Talking about why
- Telling stories
- Asking questions

This can ultimately lead to action in support of a strategy, a new culture, or an organizational change.

## HOLDING SELF AND OTHERS ACCOUNTABLE

Once you've invested in developing leadership strength, and begun to influence others to act, building in progress and accountability measures matter. As I've said many times, if the senior leaders in an organization don't align and commit to a change, that change will fail. Lasting, transformational change rarely if ever comes from the bottom up or even from the middle. Therefore, at the highest levels, senior leaders must hold themselves and others accountable if they want the rest of the organization to do the same. Remember, accountability has three components:

1. Clear goals and expectations
2. Feedback on performance against those goals and expectations
3. Rewards and consequences that align with performance against goals and expectations

## CLEAR GOALS AND EXPECTATIONS

Most organizations pick too many things to work on, say everything is a priority, and spend time firefighting instead of using disciplined focus over time. We overemphasize agility and quantity as an excuse for not doing things exceptionally well. This lack of focus filters down to individual leaders who often have a wide variety of goals (which may or may not be defined), which may work at cross purposes with vague ideas of what a good job looks like. To have accountability, you need a few clearly defined goals, where a good job is agreed upon and obvious.

Like many organizations, Luck Companies struggled with too many initiatives for years; associates would complain that leaders never took anything off the priority list. They chewed up any excess space to execute on their strategy with "side of the desk projects" and "shadow business plans." Alignment between departments varied, creating misaligned use of time and resources across the organization. The company wrote stop-doing lists and failed to stop doing anything. In 2020, the company chose focus as a leadership competency and overhauled its strategic planning and business plan processes in order to create more aligned efforts. The company stood up teams to drive clarity, accountability, and focus through resource allocation. For the first time in many years, the company wrote stop-doing lists and stopped doing things. While imperfect, the company has reduced the amount of projects it tackles in an effort to do more things exceptionally well.

### FREQUENT FEEDBACK

Like all employees, senior leaders need frequent feedback on their performance. They need positive feedback on what is going well and developmental feedback on what they can improve. Feedback is just data we can use in service of achieving goals. As children, we are awash in feedback from grades to sports teams to our parents' praise or criticism. As adults, not so much. An annual performance review is not nearly enough feedback for leaders in Values Based Organizations. We should get feedback in some form nearly every day, with more formal feedback multiple times a year. That amount of feedback gives leaders enough data to dial in their leadership and increase their effectiveness.

At Kenmore Envelope, Scott Evans and Kristin Ogo began to publicly talk about machine run times, how long changeovers took, and overall production numbers for each piece of equipment as part of their vision to outservice competitors. By making such feedback public, it encouraged adjusters to try and beat their own daily or nightly goals, speeding up changeovers and maximizing their runs. Shifts began to compete against one another for production bragging rights. Overall, the company increased envelope production and machine efficiency.

At Dcode, Meagan Metzger and her team feel strongly about giving transparent feedback. Each customer has a North Star that guides the experience their team wants to create and the goals they want to achieve. The team will then use their North Stars to guide feedback. "We use the terms 'pluses' and 'deltas.' After every client meeting, we ask, 'What are some pluses and deltas—what went well, and what didn't go well?' It makes feedback more approachable." Dcode balances high performance with high engagement. "We want our culture to be open and lighthearted and fun," which Meagan believes helps her team perform better, yet leaders also need to deliver tough, performance-driven feedback. She believes in the power of both. "The Dcode punch wouldn't go so well," as Meagan says.

### REWARDS AND CONSEQUENCES

High performance should be rewarded, and low performance should not be tolerated. However, most organizational systems do not allow us to truly differentiate high performance from mediocre performance, except through promotions. In fact, we tend to reward high performers with more work and wonder why they quit.

Rewards include all the ways we incentivize people to perform at their highest levels. Money is part of the equation, but not all.

Money is not a great long-term motivator; you will run out of money by increasing costs to the point that the organization can no longer function well. Money is also a powerful demotivator, especially if the individual feels that they are not being compensated fairly. To champion Values Based Leadership, leaders must find ways of rewarding performance beyond money.

There are many ways to ensure people feel valued in addition to money, such as key assignments, flexibility, praise, support, empathy, and public recognition. People do want to feel compensated fairly, yet they also want to feel accepted, cared about, and trusted. Rewards should encompass as many factors as possible when it comes to encouraging high performance. And individuals have their own needs, values, and assumptions. What thrills one person may feel like a slap in the face to another.

For example, Luck Companies experimented with a variety of rewards for associates who excelled at leading its values culture. At one point, the company decided to pay select hourly workers a $5,000 bonus for modeling the company's values. Yet the company had spent a decade building highly collaborative work teams. When managers awarded individuals, the associates felt appalled. Many used the checks to pay for parties for their teams, asked the managers not to announce their names, or donated the money to charity. The rewards did not match the individuals or the culture the company had built.

Consequences, on the other hand, include all the ways of correcting less than optimal performance, including developmental feedback, lack of promotions and key assignments, reduced responsibility, corrective actions, and less flexibility. Termination serves as the ultimate consequence for poor performance, but often employees can improve with the right mix of rewards and less enduring consequences. As one manager told me, "Nothing improves morale like a good firing." He was right; when we fired him, morale did improve.

Some organizations struggle with such consequences. I hear from many clients in state and federal agencies that they cannot hold people accountable because they don't have the tools to do so. If senior leaders do not have access to rewards and consequences, they will struggle to hold others accountable. Performance suffers, and highly talented employees leave. Yet we often have more tools at our disposal than we believe. My advice is to work closely with Human Resources to understand and use the available tools.

Leaders complain that HR can serve as a barrier to accountability, forcing them to retain low performers out of fear of lawsuits. More often I find that managers wait too long to get HR involved, or do not like the recordkeeping required to show how the manager handled employee performance. The manager's job is to be clear, to offer frequent feedback, and to use the reward and consequence tools they have access to. The manager's job is also to maintain records of performance, to illustrate the employee's history of performance without favoritism or bias. HR should provide a consistent process and coach managers on how to use it effectively—HR's role is to help the organization achieve its goals, in alignment with the mission, values, vision, and strategy. Like all shared service teams, HR needs to add value to the organization if they want to feel valued and included by senior leaders.

Leaders, of course, must hold themselves accountable first and foremost. By establishing clear goals, getting feedback on their performance, and accepting both rewards and discipline, leaders set the standard for others to follow. When I consider a lack of accountability by senior leaders, I am reminded of the financial crisis of 2008 when the financial institutions most responsible for the subprime mortgage meltdown enjoyed bonuses and promotions as the economy collapsed. Or when frontline staff lose their jobs from bad strategy and a lack of foresight at the senior-most levels. In these organizations, leaders undermine their own credibility going forward and will have to rebuild the commitment of their people if they desire to initiate changes going forward. Employees, perhaps nonintuitively, crave clarity and thrive in high-accountability cultures.

**KEY TAKEAWAYS**

To champion Values Based Leadership, we:

- Develop leadership strength
- Influence key people
- Hold self and others accountable

# CHAPTER SEVEN

# Engage Everyone

Why Engage Everyone?

Higher engagement leads to better results, increased support, and more actions that support the organization's goals.

Drs. Jerry and Jana Burch have traveled the world; they have seen strategy and culture work in the US Navy, in middle schools, in for-profits and nonprofits, as well as in universities. They have experienced strategies that have been led well and those that have not.

"We were in a meeting when someone asked our team, 'If you got an extra $50,000 tomorrow, what would you do with it?' Not one person in our group said, 'Wait a second, our strategy says our number one priority is this. We would spend it there.'" Jerry and Jana believe that leaders should make strategic planning as public as possible, explaining it thoroughly, and engaging everyone. "It's the kind of question that can be answered in two seconds," says Jerry, if the strategy is led well.

In their minds, strategy creates alignment, especially if it incorporates the values of an organization. "We're not going to have an argument over what you did. We're going to talk about how what you did aligns or doesn't align with our values." If you actively use your strategic plan to make decisions, you remove all the pettiness of "you win versus I win," according to Jerry. Good strategy creates space for people to communicate, build relationships, play, and avoid their ego since it provides a framework for action that supersedes our personal issues. To reach this point, you must engage everyone in the execution of the strategy, clearly describing how to use it as a framework for making decisions.

"Strategy is a tool for making decisions and for leading. If not, that's problematic," says Jana. "You're more willing to move if you are committed to the organization and the plan." If employees feel that the decisions don't align, or worse, support someone's personal agenda, the environment grows toxic. "I was teaching at a middle school, and in this main hallway we had our pillars of character," says Jana. "We walked by them every day. We had lessons drilling them into the kids. But our administration did not value those pillars and didn't demonstrate the pillars in action. It made us sour, and not talk about them. Organizational values and strategy are the same. If we only whip it out when it benefits us, it really kills morale."

As a contrast, Jerry shared a story from his days in the Navy about an exceptional Captain. "At every meeting, you were expected to talk about our values. He also held us accountable to act on them. And he expected you to hold him accountable, too." If leaders are not willing to hold themselves and others accountable to the values and the strategy, Jerry believes, "it allows everybody else to run amok. It's where a lot of our strategic plans and values fail."

Jerry and Jana compare leading strategy to Newton's law of inertia: An object in motion stays in motion. To make strategy and organizational change successful, they believe leaders should keep the organization in a state of leaning forward, ready to move in the right direction. To keep the organization in motion, leaders should keep positive pressure on the organization, avoiding complacency and stillness. As an example, they share a story of mentoring a single mother who started a house painting business to keep her family together and stay out of poverty. Then COVID-19 hit. Her instinct was to abandon her business because she did not see any way forward. Their role as mentors was to help the business owner recognize she could keep taking baby steps forward until the world came back. "We didn't ask her to move a million miles. We had a plan, we had incremental steps, and we kept in motion. She got online faster than others, and she saved her business."

Leadership is a choice, not a title; we have potential leaders at every level in our organizations. Everyone, whether they work on the shop floor, ring out customers in a restaurant, or work in a corner office, can make choices that have a positive impact on others. Moreover, their efforts can move the organization's culture forward while executing its strategy.

While the most important group of people to influence in any organizational change includes the top leaders, followed by their direct reports, then the key influencers, you still need a game plan for how to engage the rest of the organization. We want to inspire employee commitment to our mission, values, vision, and strategy and ultimately want them to take action. To do so, we need to:

- Engage leadership at all levels
- Energize employees with direction and support
- Empower employees to make a difference

For those of you who believe engaging everyone is fluffy and unnecessary, ask yourself: Who talks to your customers every day? Who works with your vendors? Who builds your products? Probably not the senior leaders; it is probably the front line of your organization. Why wouldn't you want their commitment? Sure, through mandates, money, and the occasional threat, you can cajole employees into taking action. You can get their compliance. But to earn their commitment, we need more than just carrots and sticks. We need engagement.

## ENGAGE LEADERS AT ALL LEVELS

At Luck Companies, one of the values of the organization is leadership. Luck expects every associate, from the person driving a truck the size of your house to the vice president overseeing operations across four states, to lead. For example, Luck expects associates to develop themselves and others, to inspire confidence and optimism within their teams, and to confront issues with courage and compassion. The company has spent twenty years developing the culture of the organization and the leadership capacity to do so, at every level. Additionally, Luck screens every candidate using the organization's values through online assessments and behavioral-based interview questions—ensuring that new hires want to lead and clearly understand what they are signing up for. Managers measure associate behaviors against the values through performance reviews and expect successor candidates, at both the hourly and salaried levels, to model leadership behaviors within their teams.

As a measure of the company's health, Luck Companies has used engagement surveys since the early 2000s to better understand what drives performance in the organization. Employee engagement is a well-researched measure of how employees feel about the organization, as well as if they believe they have the tools, resources, and skills to do the job. High engagement leads to more discretionary effort of employees, effort they pour into their jobs. This extra effort improves a host of performance measures, including customer service, innovation, sales, absenteeism, safety, and retention, which translates into higher revenues and organizational performance.

Luck uses the results of these surveys to develop action plans to either strengthen employee engagement or maintain it. Sometimes the result is an organization-wide focus, and sometimes the focus is at the local team or individual level. Engagement, as the company says, is not just the responsibility of formal leaders; it is the responsibility of every associate.

If I am unhappy with my coworkers and my team, my engagement will be lower. If I feel they care about me and want me to succeed, my engagement will be higher. Over the past ten years, the company's engagement scores have risen through the 80s and into the 90s—putting the company among one of the most engaged organizations in the United States and around the globe. The company has earned such high scores not through country club management, shooting everything with the money gun, and treating associates like they are on permanent vacation, but through a dedicated effort to engage leaders at all levels.

In order to engage leaders at all levels, formal leaders need to model what good leadership looks like. If they don't lead well, employees, as professional boss watchers, will see it, and will likely model the wrong behaviors as a result. It is difficult to lead well when you are not being led well. Especially when it is not safe for employees to do so.

For example, once considered a highly respected banking institution, Wells Fargo stumbled during the 2010s when it came to light that the company had opened over 3.5 million fraudulent accounts to meet its cross-selling quotas. At first, senior leaders and the board resisted accountability, focusing on the five thousand frontline employees the company fired as a result. However, over time the company paid hundreds of millions in fines while the bank's CEO resigned. After years of hearings, investigators determined that a high-pressure sales environment, financial incentives tied to cross-selling, and pressure from local, regional, and the senior leaders encouraged branch employees to forge signatures, sell bogus products, and mislead customers.

In command-and-control environments, employees worry that others will punish them for leadership behaviors like giving feedback or articulating a vision. In this case, employees have learned to be helpless—to wait to be told what to do and to keep their ideas and opinions to themselves. Fear permeates these teams, sapping great talent and opportunity. Fear keeps employees playing small—careful not to make a mistake and earn the wrath of the higher-ups. In Values Based Organizations, we need employees to play big—especially when it comes to leading others. We need to drive out fear and replace it with inspiration and confidence. We need to make it safe.

Researchers have written about psychological safety for years, but the idea grew widespread after Google studied many of its highest-performing teams and found that the teams where employees felt safe to take risks, try new things, and be vulnerable with one another had better results than the teams where the psychological safety was lower. Leaders can lower an employee's sense of psychological safety by shutting down new ideas, acting defensive when faced with feedback, or publicly humiliating those who fail. For Jana Burch, observing leaders make self-serving decisions undermined her commitment and her willingness to try new things. She did not feel safe, assuming those leaders would take advantage of her natural drive and hard work. Jerry found the opposite in the Navy, because of consistent accountability. When everyone feels accountable, it frees employees from overfocusing on fairness and personal conflict. Accountability, while seemingly paradoxical, can increase employees' sense of psychological safety. Like Harley-Davidson's use of values to build freedom with fences: employees had the freedom and expectation to innovate inside the fences of their culture.

I find that most leaders do not intend to shut down, humiliate, or take advantage of their employees, but sometimes do so because of their style or through a lack of self-awareness. Creating psychological safety does not mean that we need to walk around on eggshells with our employees. Quite the opposite. We should set high standards, inspiring others to perform at the peak of their potential. We should be open to ideas, show curiosity, and when giving others tough developmental feedback, do so with care and an authentic desire to see them flourish. Don't play small with your employees and don't expect them to play small with you.

Once we have modeled what good leadership looks like, and we have made it safe, then we need to set the expectation for all employees to lead. We cannot assume they will, and we need to help them understand that a good job includes leadership. At every level. Informal leadership—without positional power—is more difficult than formal leadership. Ever try to get a peer to do something they did not want to do? It's like trying to get a bunch of engineers to do trust fall exercises: it will probably end in tears even if nobody gets hurt.

We can define what informal leadership looks like, and then develop employee skills to do so. For example, leadership choices at all levels include:

- Developing yourself and others
- Asking for help and offering help
- Giving and getting feedback
- Adapting our approach for the person and the situation
- Articulating a vision
- Communicating effectively by asking, listening, and confirming what they hear
- Empathizing with others

None of these behaviors require position power to succeed. Anyone in your organization, with the right expectations and training, can do so. Imagine a strategy of reducing costs and increasing margins. Any employee can share ideas about how to save money or give feedback about how to make a process more efficient, or coach another employee on how to work smarter. Now imagine if every employee in the organization did these three things consistently. How could you not reduce costs and increase margins, with everyone acting to support the same goal?

### ENERGIZE EMPLOYEES WITH DIRECTION AND SUPPORT

In their book, *Management of Organizational Behavior: Utilizing Human Resources* (1969), Paul Hersey and Ken Blanchard first described their situational leadership model. After Hersey and Blanchard parted ways, Hersey continued to teach Situational Leadership and Blanchard developed Situational Leadership II. Their incredibly helpful models require leaders to adapt to the developmental level of their followers on a specific task to help them build competence and commitment to that task. As competence and commitment rise, so does performance.

New strategies, values, and leadership expectations will inevitably require employees to learn new things. In the beginning, with any new skill, people will feel awkward and may resist trying new behaviors and processes. We don't like feeling incompetent and may be jaded about why changing a process matters. To help energize employee commitment to new tasks, we should follow Hersey and Blanchard's advice: we need to provide employees with direction—tell them what to do, teach them how to do it, set expectations, and provide clarity. We should also provide support—listen, ask questions, share why, empathize when they feel frustrated, and help them learn how to solve their own problems. In general, we should vary how much direction and support we provide employees based on their ability to perform the task—higher direction in the beginning and more support in the middle. Once they have mastered a task, we still need to stay close to them, but the amount of direction and support they need is much, much lower, while their performance is much, much higher. As Bob Kelley points out, "There is a strong connection between individual behaviors and organizational outcomes."

One mistake many organizations make when launching new changes is to underestimate how much time and energy it will take to adopt new processes. The first time an employee hears about a change, they are unlikely to immediately support it. You must build their awareness, understanding, and eventually acceptance of the change before they will try new behaviors. To move them along the way, you will need to provide both direction and support. I've seen numerous IT systems put in place over the years, where the system did not fail but the organization failed to spend enough time training people. These organizations get a poorly used, less-than-optimal user base of a complicated system. It's like putting a pile of money on a table and then setting it on fire. After these failures, we love to say that people don't like change when really most managers don't like spending money, me included.

### EMPOWER EMPLOYEES TO MAKE A DIFFERENCE

The idea of empowerment has its roots in nineteenth-century political philosophies about work and labor but came into the mainstream in the 1980s and '90s in organizations. Empowerment means that employees have mastery over their own jobs, the ability to make decisions, and the resources to accomplish their goals. Empowerment, or more accurately losing control, can feel scary for managers who believe they know best, who see employees as incompetent at best and adversaries at worst. But if you want to really engage everyone, employees need to feel like they can and should contribute their efforts and their ideas. Giving employees greater autonomy to act can be a very motivational tool.

Empowerment involves risk, of course: some employees can't be trusted with more autonomy. If this is the case, how can you trust them with your customers or your expensive equipment? Another risk is that operationally efficient processes like assembly lines are designed to be consistent, not to be fiddled with. The process in this case eliminates autonomy. However, savvy managers can find ways to empower employees to make decisions—whether through quality control efforts, cross-training others, or coming up with ideas on how to further optimize processes.

Empowerment requires competence: if employees make decisions, they need the knowledge and experience to make good ones. Failure is a powerful teacher in this case—we want employees to explore and experiment, and we can make it okay for them to try new things, to learn what worked and what didn't, and then innovate. You can make mistakes, just don't make the same mistakes twice.

In my experience, everyone wants some control over their lives—few people act completely passive. It makes sense to find ways to empower employees, looking for opportunities where the value is high, the risk is low, and the effort to do so is low to moderate. What decisions can you involve them in related to the strategy you want to execute, and the culture you want to create? What decisions can you delegate to them because they have the competence they need to make great decisions? What will you give up to make space for others to play bigger?

**KEY TAKEAWAYS**

To Engage Everyone, we:

- Engage leadership at all levels
- Energize employees with direction and support
- Empower employees to make a difference

# CHAPTER EIGHT

# Putting It All Together

Why does using all of the Five Practices of Values Based Organizations matter?

The practices are interdependent; using them all together increases an organization's effectiveness.

Scott Evans, CEO, and Kristin Ogo, COO, of Kenmore Envelope, have built a company culture on the values of reputation, passion, community, drive, and safety. When he started in the business, Scott found a company that was the best manufacturer in its niche market of specialty envelopes, surrounded by competitors who had better relationships, faster growth, and higher production than Kenmore. He found employees who did not want to cross-train or do different jobs, who resisted making last-minute changes in the name of customer service. "The equipment base was there, and people worked hard, but the work and the customers were not there." That recognition inspired Scott on his journey to build something different.

Soon joined by Kristin, Scott went on the road telling Kenmore's story in different markets, spoiling his clients, and outservicing his competitors. Scott asked himself, "How can I make these envelopes, not a very sexy or cool thing, fun?" The challenge then became bringing the rest of the company along for the ride.

The two executives understand that leadership starts at the top and that emotions are contagious. "It doesn't matter what challenges may be happening today; when Scott has a can-do attitude, we all do," says Kristin. "And that makes me happy." They knew they needed to infuse their enthusiasm, sense of teamwork, and inspiration throughout the company. To start, Scott and Kristin modeled his philosophy of speed wins: they walk fast and work faster. Scott asked his teams to try new things and inspired them by sharing why it felt exciting to shift and adapt to customer priorities. They both worked to build community within their teams through friendly competition. Kristin published production records on each piece of machinery, which motivated the operators to excel. They pushed the limits of their equipment past what others could do as a result. And they did it enthusiastically. "If we can't have fun, people aren't going to stay around," says Scott. "And talent embraces the hard stuff."

As the company grew, and the culture started to change, Scott and Kristin realized they needed to build a leadership team that matched their vision for the company. According to Scott, "There are some Fortune 50s out there that think you've got to hire a bunch of assholes and scare people into performing. We wanted to have a team that fights for each other and supports one another, that cares for one another and has a good time together." As a result, they promote leaders who can run the business, work together, have fun, and still win. "It's no different than life," says Scott. "We've been through it together, the thick and thin. I don't look at it any different than family. We win together, we grow together."

Recruiting for the culture matters as well. Scott and Kristin look for employees who have grit, have a fire in their bellies to succeed, care about their craft, and want to work in teams. They want "difference makers." If you recruit difference makers, however, you must involve them. "Everyone loves to problem solve," says Kristin. "Nobody wants to be told what to do, especially if it changes their day. There's nothing worse than stuffing something down someone's throat." And so, they turned their difference makers loose on Kenmore's challenges and watched them thrive.

Walking the shop floor, between printing presses and huge rolls of paper, it is easy to see the impact of leadership on the culture. "When somebody comes in and wants to put in their résumé, they say it looks like we like each other." The two often get feedback that visitors love coming into their factory and seeing how happy people feel. It sets the tone for their visits. "I think our energy and passion come through," says Scott. "They want to be part of our team."

The Five Practices of Values Based Organizations are practical above all; these are not just steps to transforming an organization in theory, but actionable practices organizations can use to create greater alignment between culture and strategy.

**As a reminder, we will use the following definitions:**

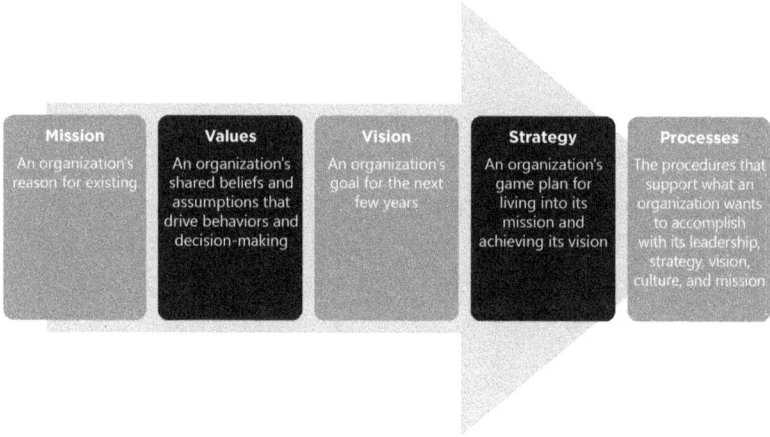

| Mission | Values | Vision | Strategy | Processes |
|---------|--------|--------|----------|-----------|
| An organization's reason for existing | An organization's shared beliefs and assumptions that drive behaviors and decision-making | An organization's goal for the next few years | An organization's game plan for living into its mission and achieving its vision | The procedures that support what an organization wants to accomplish with its leadership, strategy, vision, culture, and mission |

To illustrate these practices in action, the following is the real story of one such Values Based Organization.

The Law Family Companies, founded in 1882, is a sixth-generation family business based in Nashua, New Hampshire. The company has trucking terminals throughout the northeastern United States, alongside warehouses, moving and storage, and real estate. Before working with InnerWill, the company had budgets and a board of directors, but no annual business plan or strategy. The different business units of the company did not work closely together (except for a few instances) and did not share a single approach to planning for the future. The business faced pressures related to the COVID-19 pandemic in 2020, as well as competition in all facets of the organization.

## CHAMPION VALUES BASED LEADERSHIP

While there is a natural progression to the Five Practices, the Chief Executive Officer, Brian Law, started his efforts to align the organization by working on himself first, through executive coaching and feedback. One of the main ideas of Values Based Leadership is that if we want to make any changes in our organizations, the senior leaders must go first. And in this case, Brian did, working with a business coach on his leadership, relationships, and executive choices. After getting feedback and spending several months on his own development, he moved on to the next step of his plan.

Brian had a vision for bringing the business, the board, and even his family together in a more seamless way. To do so, he initiated a three-pronged approach: developing a family council in the family, doing strategic planning in the business, and reimagining the board in support of both.

For the business, Brian considered which senior leaders within the organization to involve in strategic planning. He chose formal leaders in each of the major business lines, who for the most part had never taken part in strategic planning or making decisions for the enterprise. Brian wanted these leaders to understand their impact on the whole business, and to enlist their help in influencing the rest of the employees. He also wanted to develop them as a team—using the strategic planning process to forge a new group of leaders. For the first time, this group came together as an executive leadership team and set out to chart the course of the business over the next three years.

Before the strategic planning process kicked off, Brian had to build a case for why it mattered. He painted a picture of why the process was necessary, what it was meant to accomplish, and the steps along the way. The group felt skeptical at first—they did not make joint decisions and worried if they could do so. They hesitated to allow other leaders to see into their business—for good or for bad—and worried about losing control. However, some of the executives felt hungry to start the work and wished they had done it years before. Despite the reservations, and building on those "chomping at the bit to be working on it," Brian persisted and moved to enact his vision.

## TAKE STOCK

In their first session, Brian and his team walked through the overarching strategic planning process that included several sessions spread out over the course of a few months. The process allowed the team to strengthen their relationships, collect data, understand their customers, and complete their due diligence homework in between sessions. After working through the high-level process, the team conducted a SWOT analysis of the business. They asked and answered the following questions:

- What are the company's overall strengths?
- What are the company's overall weaknesses?
- What are the company's opportunities?
- What are the threats to the company?

The SWOT analysis was not intended to be perfect or complete; rather, it was meant to identify high-level issues the company's strategy should address. For example, one of the company's strengths was its customer service and willingness to go the extra mile for clients (very helpful in a trucking company). Unfortunately, one of the company's weaknesses was that the company did not always get paid for these extra services—which represented a significant amount of costs and lost revenue. The company also had the opportunity to grow—to secure additional trucking terminals, warehouse space, and moving and storage crews. But in the world of trucking, finding enough operators who cared about safety and service proved difficult at the best of times. The entire industry struggles to attract younger workers, meaning many of the drivers were close, if not past, retirement age.

The team then had to identify potential ways to leverage the company's strengths, improve on its weaknesses, take advantage of opportunities, and protect against threats. They understood that service was an important part of why customers did business with the company; it was their secret sauce. Yet the company needed to overhaul how it accounted for this extra service and put in place processes that captured the extra work employees did taking care of clients. They also identified several potential acquisition targets. They knew that they would need a team to regularly review opportunistic chances to invest in other businesses and locations. Finally, the team identified succession and recruiting as a key part of the success of all the business units going forward.

As the team worked, four key strategic themes emerged from the discussion: growth, operations, people, and innovation. These themes became the company's high-level strategic objectives.

After the first session, the team tackled their homework to confirm the SWOT by interviewing customers—What did they like about the company? What could the company improve? What opportunities did they see for the company in the future? What should the company's priorities be going forward? These customer interviews could have taken place before the SWOT. However, the participants had never worked on a strategic plan before or spent time together as a leadership team. They needed experience working together first, which led to better conversations with customers.

### ALIGN ACTION

During the second session, Brian and the team identified potential tactics that supported each of the four strategic objectives. Given the differences in the business units, the team chose tactics specific to some business units and not others, while some tactics would apply to everyone. For example, each business unit needed to review its pricing, yet each had different approaches to growth. The trucking company could add terminals, drivers, and trucks, the warehouse could secure more storage capacity, and the moving and storage company could add more crews. They also discussed their findings from talking to customers, which helped them confirm their strategic objectives and solidify potential tactics.

After the second session, the team further refined their tactics and identified potential metrics, or key performance indicators, for each of their strategic objectives. The Chief Finance Officer developed a potential budget and forecast for the next three years while giving the executives a look back on their financials.

During the third session, Brian and his team agreed on the metrics for each of the strategic objectives, focusing on the few key measures they would use to guide the business such as top-line revenue growth and margin increases. They set realistic revenue and margin goals for the coming years by reviewing the forecast and previous financials. They also developed a talent plan forecasting what staffing they should recruit in support of the new strategy.

## COMMIT TO WHY AND HOW

During the fourth session, Brian and his executive team wrote the first draft of their organizational mission, or why the organization exists, as well as their values—how they would make decisions and treat others. In writing their values and supporting behaviors, they focused on straightforward, actionable language their employees could understand and act upon. They also wrote a vision—a Big Hairy Audacious Goal—that captured the spirit of the strategy. They could have completed the vision earlier in the process; however, with the strategic objectives identified, the organizational vision evolved naturally.

The homework for this fourth session was to complete their individual business unit budgets and forecasts, edit the mission, vision, and values language, and come prepared to make final decisions about their strategy.

During the fifth session, the executive team presented their portion of the strategy for feedback and input from the other members of the team. They identified processes they would need to update to better fit the organization's strategy and create more alignment between businesses. They also discussed a rollout plan and how to gather input and feedback from key stakeholders in the organization.

## ENGAGE EVERYONE

As part of the feedback loop and influence process, Brian and his team presented the rough draft of their strategy to the board, gathering their feedback and input. The board spent time identifying how they would need to evolve in better alignment with the organization's strategy and the needs of the shareholders, including putting governance processes in place like term limits and board assessments. Finally, the board decided to recruit new directors with the knowledge, skills, and abilities that would provide benefits for the organization.

The final step Brian took with his executive team included rolling out the strategy to the organization. With team leaders and key influencers, they shared the overarching strategy, the tactics supporting the strategic objectives, the values and culture the leaders wanted to create over the coming years, and what actions they would need to support the strategy going forward. He also invited the group to offer feedback and to reflect on how the strategy impacted them and their roles. Brian had each member of his leadership team present the parts of the strategy they were responsible for as a way of modeling alignment and creating public accountability for the plan.

In order to improve the execution of the strategy going forward, Brian and his team would meet at least once a quarter to discuss the business's performance in support of the strategy, how major projects progressed, and the company's work toward achieving the key performance indicators.

## TAKE STOCK, AGAIN

Strategies are not set in stone; the practices of Values Based Organizations don't happen once but work together again and again over time. Taking Stock is one such example.

As time went on, Brian and his leadership team reflected on what worked and what did not as they pursued the strategy they developed. Some tactics worked well, others did not. As Brian describes it, his "tale of woe" resulted from a shift in the economy. At the launch of the strategy, the market, which had been hot for trucking and logistics, cooled as the economy grew rockier. Manufacturing caught up to the demand that skyrocketed during COVID-19, which meant many companies had warehouses overstocked with product, resulting in a decline in shipping. Businesses pulled back on spending, while sectors cut back on costs such as moving and storage. Achieving the financial metrics laid out in the strategy became more difficult across the organization, while the strategy itself remained directionally correct.

Like any strategic plan, the Law Family Companies' strategic plan is a living document, meant to be adapted and adjusted as conditions change. These living documents follow the strong opinions, weakly held approach: they represent your organization's strong opinion about the future, and when reality proves you wrong, you shift your approach. In this case, Brian had to provide clarity to the organization and lead it to adapt. As mentioned previously, Taking Stock, like the Five Practices, is not one-and-done; it is a practice organizations engage in many times. Brian and his executive team had to Take Stock again as they monitored the health of the organization and chose a new path.

Brian's story illustrates the practical use of the Five Practices to align strategy and culture. Along with his wife, daughter, and extended family, he used a similar approach when working to establish a family council—Taking Stock of the family, Committing to Why and How as they identified their family's values, Aligning Action by putting together a plan to strengthen the family's relationships over time, Championing Values Based Leadership by developing each other and the next generation of the family, and Engaging Everyone by incorporating the voices of different family members into their plan. In developing the Law Family Companies' Board of Directors, he approached the work the same way: they Took Stock of the strengths and opportunities of the board, Committed to Why and How by clarifying the purpose of the board, Aligned Action by identifying how the board could best achieve its purpose and adopting practices that allowed the board to do so, Championing Values Based Leadership by encouraging the directors to work together more effectively, and Engaging Everyone by bringing in a facilitator to help all voices be heard as the board reimagined its future.

When led well, the Five Practices of Values Based Organizations create alignment between an organization's strategy and culture. They provide a process that ensures senior leaders have the right conversations about the future, not just developing a plan that sits on a shelf beside all the other unused plans, but a process that brings the people with the will and the skill to chart a path for the organization's future. No processes or practices guarantee success; the leadership of the people in the room does that if they have the tenacity and influence to see that these practices move beyond just a flavor-of-the-month approach to strategic planning and into a way of doing business that lasts. These practices represent an investment in time and energy and harness a commonsense approach to getting the organization moving in the same direction.

Our organizations are the greatest resource we have for making a positive difference in the world. Why not harness the talents of our employees and take them on a journey that does more than generate revenue, that ensures our organizations do not just survive but thrive, providing jobs, development, paychecks, opportunity, and community. The Five Practices of Values Based Organizations have their roots in this mission—to develop better people, braver leaders, and a wiser world through the strength of our organizations.

**KEY TAKEAWAYS**

To follow the Five Practices of Values Based Organizations, we:

- Take Stock
- Commit to Why and How
- Align Action
- Champion Values Based Leadership
- Engage Everyone

# Epilogue

Imagine the gears in an engine, out of alignment, grinding together, missing and spitting and jerking the car to a halt.

Imagine a group of rowers, all pulling at different speeds and in different directions.

Imagine an orchestra where the players play different songs at different tempos and volumes while the conductor is nowhere to be seen.

Imagine a sports team where everyone follows a different playbook and doesn't understand what position they play.

These images describe the typical organization: unclear on where they are going, why they are going there, and what they want to accomplish.

Now imagine an organization that has a clear mission explaining why it exists. Whose culture supports the outcomes of its strategic plan. Whose vision inspires employees to think big and work toward a common goal. An organization with leaders who model similar behaviors, actively influence teams to work together, and despite having strong opinions publicly commit to the organization's goals. Processes that make sense, that enable the culture, strategy, and leaders. An organization with employees who understand their goals, who act on the values of the organization, and contribute to something larger than themselves, every day.

This is an untypical organization. Rare, even unicorn-like. Having this level of extreme alignment is possible, but it takes leadership and influence, hard work and processes. It takes people with the will and skill to see the alignment through, who don't settle for mediocrity, who don't make excuses, who focus on a few priorities and don't tolerate terrible leaders to run roughshod across their teams.

You wouldn't build an engine that misfires constantly, or field a sports team that had no positions, or listen to an orchestra playing different songs in different keys simultaneously. So why do we settle for organizations that have no stated mission, no clear goals for the future, and no plan to get there other than do more with less but faster? Organizations whose culture holds them hostage, and keeps them from achieving greatness? Organizations whose leaders couldn't hit water if they fell out of a boat? And employees so disengaged they drag their feet counting the minutes to quitting time, then retirement?

Our organizations don't have to be this way. We can choose a different path, a path that runs in a straight line between mission to values, vision to strategy, leadership to process. We can build organizations that make sense. Organizations that run well.

And it all starts with a choice; your choice.

# Select References

Blanchard, K. & O'Connor, M. (1996). *Managing By Values: How to Put Your Values Into Action for Extraordinary Results*. Berrett-Koehler Publishers.

Blanchard, K., Zigarmi, P. & Zigarmi, D. (2013). *Leadership and the One Minute Manager: Increasing Effectiveness Through Situational Leadership II*. William Morrow.

Epperson, T. (2022). *InnerWill: Developing Better People, Braver Leaders, and a Wiser World Through the Practice of Values Based Leadership*. InnerWill Media.

Ford (2007). *Code of Conduct Handbook*.

Heath, C. & Heath, D. (2010). *Switch: How to Change Things When Change Is Hard*. Crown Currency.

Hersey, P. & Blanchard, K. (1969). *Management of Organizational Behavior: Utilizing Human Resources*. Prentice Hall.

Kim, W. & Mauborgne, R. (2015). *Blue Ocean Strategy: How to Create Uncontested Market Space and Make the Competition Irrelevant*. Harvard Business Review Press.

Kondo, M. (2014). *The Life-Changing Magic of Tidying Up: The Japanese Art of Decluttering and Organizing*. Ten Speed Press.

Kouzes, J. & Posner, B. (2023). *The Leadership Challenge: How to Make Extraordinary Things Happen in Organizations.* Jossey-Bass.

Margretta, J. (2011). *Understanding Michael Porter: The Essential Guide to Competition and Strategy.* Harvard Business Review Press.

Porter, Michael E. (2008). "The Five Competitive Forces that Shape Strategy." *Special Issue on HBS Centennial. Harvard Business Review* 86, no. 1 (January 2008): 78-93.

Osterwalder, A. & Pigneur, Y. (2010). *Business Model Generation: A Handbook for Visionaries, Game Changers, and Challengers.* John Wiley and Sons.

Tesla (2018). *The Anti-Handbook Handbook.*